TWAYNE'S WORLD AUTHORS SERIES

A Survey of the World's Literature

Sylvia E. Bowman, Indiana University

GENERAL EDITOR

SPAIN

ity

GONZALO de BERCEO

by John Esten Keller

This first critical and historical study in English of the entirety of Gonzalo de Berceo's works brings together the salient aspects of the thirteenth-century poet's life and writing. The author investigates at length the important *Milagros de Nuestra Senora* and the well-known *Vidas,* but space is also devoted to the minor works, several of which have been accorded almost no modern critical evaluation.

Berceo's reasons for writing are seriously assessed according to the most recent arguments and theories, some of which vary considerably from earlier ideas. Berceo's life is a mystery, almost no information about him having survived, but the man may be seen in his works and in his very tangible attempts to establish rapport with his public.

Dr. Keller has set the life and work of his subject against the historical and literary backgrounds of his time.

TWAYNE'S WORLD AUTHORS SERIES (TWAS)

The purpose of TWAS is to survey the major writers—novelists, dramatists, historians, poets, philosophers, and critics—of the nations of the world. Among the national literatures covered are those of Australia, Canada, China, Eastern Europe, France, Germany, Greece, India, Italy, Japan, Latin America,˙ New Zealand, Poland, Russia, Scandinavia, Spain, and the African nations, as well as Hebrew, Yiddish, and Latin Classical literatures. This survey is complemented by Twayne's United States Authors Series and English Authors Series.

The intent of each volume in these series is to present a critical-analytical study of the works of the writer; to include biographical and historical material that may be necessary for understanding, appreciation, and critical appraisal of the writer; and to present all material in clear, concise English—but not to vitiate the scholarly content of the work by doing so.

Gonzalo de Berceo

By JOHN ESTEN KELLER

University of Kentucky

GONZALO de BERCEO

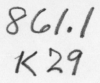
To Nicholson Barney Adams
who showed the way

Preface

Gonzalo de Berceo certainly occupies a very important niche in the pantheon of Spanish writers. His is chronologically the first name to appear in the annals of Spanish literature, although he was not, of course, the first to write Spanish literature, as the earlier anonymous masterpiece the *Poem of the Cid* testifies. His favorite verse form, the *cuaderna via* (fourfold way), made up of monorhymed quatrains, was used by other poets in the thirteenth century and in the fourteenth and was the vehicle of major literary documents. Some think he invented this form of narrative verse, but whether he did or not matters not as much as the enormous impetus he probably imparted to *cuaderna via,* for it was regarded during and after his time as the best vehicle for the poetry of the *mester de clerecía* (the school of erudite poetry).

Until the last few decades Berceo's works were studied primarily as examples of pious writings in the vernacular, or were the subject of research in medieval Spanish vocabulary, syntax, style and linguistic structure, while some scholars investigated his writings for themes and motifs, or for elements of daily life and custom in the thirteenth century. Still others have labored hard to unravel his intent as a writer, his rapport with his contemporaries, his allegory, and his symbolism.

Berceo's subject matter, since it was ecclesiastical—the miracles of saints and of the Blessed Virgin or having to do with visions and asceticism—lay well within the realm of specialized interests, and too few scholars read him for his poetic qualities. Berceo is not, it must be admitted, as fine a poet as Juan Ruiz, the Archpriest of Hita, nor one as sophisticated as Alfonso el Sabio and the better representatives of the Galician-Portuguese lyric school, nor was he skillful or gifted enough in handling certain important literary motifs, for example, the "Faust-theme," to produce a truly classic treatment of such motifs.

Notwithstanding all this, Berceo has in recent years emerged as "a charming primitive," and is once more the subject of critical and scholarly study. New and better editions of his writings are appearing. His style and his art are being scrutinized anew and are subjected to modern literary approaches. His sources, known for years, are now being reexamined in an effort to detect more that is original and, with him personal, and his very milieu, better known to us through historical, archaeological and anthropological studies, is being assessed more carefully. The results of all this investigation and renewed interest have already contributed valuable new concepts about him, his work, his times, and his contemporaries.

Behind the ingenuous façade of a simple parish priest, blindly devoted to the Blessed Virgin and to his local saints—and he was indeed so devoted—there begins to emerge a personage of greater depth, deeper wisdom, broader knowledge, and greater literary originality and skill. Berceo can be seen as a writer of many facets—a collector of literary and folk miracles, a researcher of documents calculated to shape and mold certain aspects of medieval Spanish society, and perhaps above all as a gifted, even a talented, spinner of tales, of stories skillfully spun out for a larger number of reasons than had been originally suspected.

Actually, it should not be surprising that Berceo's works still have the power to interest us today just as they interested readers in the thirteenth century. People, even in our own century of disbelief and doubt, when some go so far as to insist that God is dead, can still be moved by this Castilian poet, who obviously believed the stories he told. Those who still have credence in divine intervention—and many still do, especially in rural areas and in the region where Berceo flourished—can find pleasure and comfort in Berceo's works. People who still feel some emotion when they read or listen to such stories as *Our Lady's Juggler* by Anatole France, or Bécquer's *The Organist,* or one of the scores of versions of that wonderful old story of the Virgin's substitution for the runaway nun, can be impressed by Berceo, this thirteenth-century poet. Only a few of his brief narratives have been translated into English, unfortunately.

Gonzalo de Berceo is not a complete biography of the poet, for too many facts about his life are denied us. Nor is this book an attempt to offer a definitive critical appraisal of the rather sizable corpus of his writings. Rather it is designed to be a general survey of his life, his times and his writings, as well as of the place Berceo occupied in the development of medieval Spanish literature. This study is based upon most of the significant scholarship on Berceo to date—books, articles, monographs, etc., and upon certain opinions of my own which have crystallized through some years of perusing

Preface

Berceo's works. It is, I believe, the first such general and comprehensive study in English of Spain's first known literary figure.

JOHN ESTEN KELLER

Lexington, Kentucky

I wish to express gratitude to members of my family and to friends and colleagues who have contributed their patience, knowledge, and encouragement to the writing of this book. Special thanks goes to my wife Dinsmore and to my daughter Laurie and son Jack who often had to put up with me as I stole hours away from family life so as to give time to a thirteenth-century Spanish poet. Special thanks, too, are given to Helen Farmer, who, as my Administrative Assistant in the School of Letters and Languages of the University of Kentucky, smoothed the way for scholarship, taking upon herself many of the burdens that I should have carried. Dr. Brian Dutton of the University of Georgia while I was writing the book, and now Chairman of the Department of Romance Languages at Chicago Circle, gave me unstintedly of his advice and knowledge, and I thank him for it gratefully. Nicholson B. Adams, friend and mentor across a lifetime, inspired and stimulated me throughout my labors for which no gratitude can compensate him adequately.

For financial assistance—a grant for a research assistant and funds for typing—I thank the Kentucky Research Foundation and make it known that without such help the book would have been much slower in its writing and preparation.

Acknowledgment is made to the Editors of Tamesis Books for their kind permission to quote from Brian Dutton's *La Vida de San Millán de la Cogolla* and to the Editors of Dell's Laurel Masterpieces of World Literature for quotations from *Medieval Age*. The scholarly articles, books, monographs, and studies which were used are too numerous to mention here, but to all that helped me as I wrote *Gonzalo de Berceo* I tender thanks and appreciation.

Last but not least, I give thanks to Dr. Joseph R. Jones of the Department of Spanish and Italian Languages and Literatures of the University of Kentucky for his kindness and his expertise in reading the typescript and for his detailed and careful criticism of it.

Chronology

409   End of Roman rule in Spain: the Peninsula is overrun by Alans, Suevi, and Vandals.

456   After four decades of strife the Visigoths rule in Spain.

574   Death of St. Aemilianus.

636   Death of St. Isidore of Seville.

646   Death of St. Braulius (Braulio, author of *Life of Blessed Aemilianus*).

654   Hispano-Roman and Visigothic laws fused in *Forum Judicum* (*Laws of the Judges*).

711   Islamic invasion led by Tarik: Fall of the Kingdom of the Visigoths.

718   Battle of Covadonga, a Christian victory: Beginning of the Reconquest.

778   Charlemagne invades Spain. French disaster at the Pass of Roncesvalles.

791   Oviedo made capital of Asturias.

1000   Birth of Santo Domingo de Silos.

1002   The army of Almanzor burns the Monastery of San Millán.

1030   Relics of St. Aemilianus interred at Monastery of San Millán.

1040 or 1041   Santo Domingo leaves priorship of San Millán to become Abbot of Silos.

1069   Death of Santa Oria.

1073   Santo Domingo dies.

1085   Toledo falls to Alfonso VI of Castile and Leon.

1086–1148   Almoravides reunite Moorish Andalusia.

1099   Death of the Cid.

1146   Almohades invade Andalusia.

1197 or 1198   Birth of Gonzalo de Berceo.

1212   Christians defeat Moslems decisively at Las Navas de Tolosa.

1214   Death of Alfonso VIII and accession of Ferdinand III.

1236   Ferdinand III takes Moorish Cordova.

1246 or thereabouts   Berceo dies.

CHAPTER 1

Berceo's Spain

GONZALO de Berceo seems to have lived far-removed from the stirring life of thirteenth-century Spain and from the events that shaped its history. This did not, of course, prevent Berceo from filling his works with local color and with daily life as he saw these facets of human activity. Like other medieval writers, he used scenes, costumes, and customs of his own day to set the background of his writings. Therefore, it is characteristic to find the sixth-century St. Aemilianus portrayed by Berceo as a thirteenth-century cleric. In the contemporary secular *Crónica Troyana (Trojan Chronicle)* one finds the same interesting phenomenon, for Greeks and Trojans of pre-Classical times fight like medieval soldiers and wear armor worn by men of the thirteenth century. All of us, of course, have witnessed this phenomenon in the canvasses of Leonardo da Vinci and Michelangelo, in which we view the Apostles and others who inhabited the Palestine of Jesus' day, clothed in the raiment of the Renaissance and moving through the porticoes and piazzas of Italy. Just as an understanding of da Vinci's training and milieu enhances our enjoyment of his paintings, so an understanding of Berceo's Spain makes reading him more pleasant and rewarding. Since the poet enables us to savor the times in which he lived, because he insisted on drawing elements of those times into his works, some short treatment of the Spain of Berceo should be presented, even though one can enjoy his poems without such treatment, just as one not initiated into the history of the Greece of Homer, can enjoy the *Iliad* and the *Odyssey*.

Every one in thirteenth-century Spain, depending upon social position and education, understood to a greater or lesser degree that Rome had been the ancient mother of Spaniards. Roman roads, repaired periodically by Spanish rulers and churchmen, traversed the Peninsula, Roman ruins—arches, amphitheatres, baths, columns, and even entire buildings, some still usable—dotted the landscape. Segovia's vast aqueduct soared, as it does to this day,

15

above that city's streets. Reminders, then, of the Roman heritage, both in its pagan and its Christian aspects, were ever present and ever visible. Berceo probably stored drinking water in Roman amphoras to be found scattered about the fields and farmlands. He, like all who read history, sensed the importance of a Roman heritage that went back to Antiquity. And postclassical Roman culture, fostered and preserved by the living Church of Berceo's day, served further, of course, to keep the Roman way bright in medieval Spanish eyes.[1]

Although Berceo must have believed in and proudly accepted the Visigothic heritage which had gone far to replace the Roman, he surely realized that no matter how strong in battle and no matter how influential in the medieval way of Spanish life had been the Visigoths, Spain owed no great debt to their culture and civilization. After all, they had had no written language of their own and perforce had used Latin for all their records, whether historical, ecclesiastical, or literary. Indeed, some of Berceo's works rested upon Latin documents penned in Visigothic times.[2]

Spanish pride in the Visigothic tradition lay in other areas of human life. There was the knowledge that from Visigothic rulers had sprung the noble houses of the Spanish kingdoms. These rulers, supported by their Hispano-Roman subjects, had defended the land against the Moslem invasion from Africa in the eighth century, and though they had been defeated in the year 711, and though large areas of the Peninsula had lain under Islamic domination for centuries, and indeed still lay to some extent under this rule in Berceo's time, Spaniards continued to look with respect and fondness on the glorious days of the Goths.

Berceo knew, like all Spaniards, that the last Visigothic king, Roderick, had been slain in a great battle against the Moors who had then conquered all Spain. He knew, too, that a few chosen officers and churchmen, together with their families and retinues, had slipped out of Roderick's capital, Toledo, to flee northward, taking shelter in the mountain fastnesses of Asturias. Pelayo, the leader of this important although small band of refugees, had been able to defeat the Moslems at the Battle of Covadonga in 718, just seven years after the Moslem invasion. Pelayo in this decisive battle initiated the Reconquest which would continue through Berceo's lifetime and which would end with the final defeat of Spanish Islam at Granada in 1492.

In Berceo's day Spain, then, was still a divided land, even though the Moor had been driven back and confined to Andalusia. The North, the vast central plateau, and parts of the South were under Christian rule. But parts of Andalusia, which contained great and important cities like Málaga and Granada, remained the cradle and center of Spanish Islam and of Moslem civilization in Spain. Allied to Morocco, and even to more distant Mohammedan centers of power, The Kingdom of Granada still posed a danger to her Christian neighbors.[3] Two centuries later, Ferdinand and Isabella would have to turn aside from their plans of exploration and expansion to stamp out once and for all the Moslem presence in their realm. Berceo could very well have traveled to Moorish Spain, for there were times of peace and truce. Total war between people who have coexisted for centuries and who had come to share many customs and habits and ways of life, cannot continue for hundreds of years without some interruption. Periods of truce came and went, and while armies did not move and politicians did not plot, frontiers were open to various kinds of peaceful intercourse. Merchants crossed the borders, scholars and artists exchanged cultural ideas, diplomats and their families and staffs became commonplace in the separate sides of the frontier.[4] In short, most of the facets of Christian and Islamic Spanish life merged, and the one influenced the other. In actuality, the periods of peace were longer than the periods of war, and if we tend to forget this, the fault lies with historians whose attention to matters military and political is usually closer than to the affairs of peace. Those who inhabited the two sides of the border adapted their lives to both peace and war, as did the many who yearned to cross the frontier to see how people lived on the other side. But if Berceo ever went into Moslem Spain, he was unable to overcome his prejudices. To him, if we may judge by the content of his works and by his comments about Moorish character, the Moslem was a villainous creature, dangerous, treacherous, and ever ready to persecute unhappy Christian captives. One can doubt with reason that he ever went to Andalusia and that he ever had an opportunity to observe the life of alien people beyond the frontier.

Berceo could rest assured, although suspicion and fear dies slowly, that the Cross would eventually defeat the Crescent in Spain. Not even the great Moorish victory at Alarcos in 1195, which occurred just prior to Berceo's birth and of which he, as a child, would have heard mentioned repeatedly, could alter the inevitable. Sultan Yucub, who defeated the Spaniards at Alarcos in that year, had not taken advantage of the victory and had returned to Morocco. In 1212, just seventeen years after Alarcos, the armies of Castile, Navarre, and Aragon, led by Alfonso VIII of Castile, crushingly defeated the Moslem at Las Navas de Tolosa and delivered what may be considered as the *coup de grâce* to Islamic hopes in the Peninsula. At this time Berceo was fourteen or fifteen years old. It must have been apparent to him that the Moorish threat was on the wane.

Two important kingdoms in Spain, Castile and Leon, were fused in the thirteenth century. King Alfonso VIII died in 1214, leaving as his heir and as new king his eleven-year-old son, Ferdinand III. This remarkable young king, guided for a few years by counsellors and by his mother Queen Berenguela, became one of the most powerful monarchs in the Middle Ages. Dubbed by his people Fernando el Santo (Ferdinand the Saint), for his holy wars against Islam, he all but completed the Christian conquest of the Peninsula. The greatest of all Moorish cities in Spain, Cordova, fell to Ferdinand's armies in 1236, only a few years before Berceo's death. King Ferdinand's son, to rule as Alfonso X,[5] helped the king to capture Seville in 1248 and was himself the general who captured Murcia. In 1248 also, Ferdinand's brother, James of Aragon, took Valencia and the Balearic Islands. In Berceo's lifetime, then, most of the Moorish domination ended. Only the Kingdom of Granada stood.

Literary activity in Berceo's time was considerable. Lyric poetry, though not well represented in the thirteenth century, insofar as Castilian is concerned, nonetheless existed. What has obscured the early Castilian lyric is this: the learned poets, those whose works would have been most likely to survive, preferred as the vehicle for poetic expression, not Castilian, but rather a dialect of Portuguese known as Galician. King Alfonso himself wrote many poems in Galician, as did some two hundred poets whose names have survived the ages.[6] Berceo might not have had reason to read or hear recited the poems of great and noble poets like Prince Alfonso, but he would certainly have heard the lyrics of the common people, from whom, incidentally, a considerable number of courtly poets drew inspiration. Berceo himself, it will be seen later, attempted lyric verse, although little of what he wrote in this genre has survived.

Epic, or at least epic-type poetry, recited by bards from time immemorial, lived on surely in Berceo's day. The variety we regard as of folkloristic origin, known as the *mester de juglaría* (minstrel's school) was the vehicle of the famous *Cantar de Mio Cid (Lay of My Cid)*, a lengthy narrative poem almost certainly sung as late as the thirteenth century and quite probably heard by Berceo from the mouth of some *juglar* (minstrel).[7] This poetry was of irregular verses although the basic pattern was for lines of sixteen syllables, with two hemistichs each of eight syllables divided by a caesura or pause. Assonance, or vowel rhyme, was another important feature. Such poetry was becoming old-fashioned in Berceo's time.

Other literary pieces which must have been written in the *mester de juglaría* were the numerous epic-type poems, whose names survive, but whose poetic form has been lost. Only in prosification have such old narrative themes as the *Siete Infantes de Lara (Seven Princes of Lara)*, the *Cantar de Rodrigo (Song of Rodrigo)*, the *Cerco de Zamora (Siege of Zamora)*, and the *Cantar de Bernardo del Carpio (Song of Bernardo del Carpio)* lived on.[8] Shorter poems, believed to belong to the *mester de juglaría* due to their similar poetic form, could have been heard recited by Berceo: *La Vida de Santa María Egipcíaca (Life of St. Mary the Egyptian)*, *El Libro dels Tres Reis d'Orient (Book of the Three Kings from the Orient)* are two.

Debates, also considered as belonging to the *mester de juglaría*, were in vogue in Berceo's time, and even thereafter. Long popular in Latin, debates were adapted to the vernaculars for poetic expression, and Spanish was no exception. Two characters, which might be human beings or abstract personifications like Love, Death, or Wine and Water, argue. The more famous ones in Spanish are *Disputa del Alma e el Cuerpo (Dispute of the Soul and the Body)*, the *Denuestos del Agua e el Vino (Reproaches of Water and Wine)*, and *Elena e María (Helen and Mary)*.[9] In each the characters in the title argue. Such debates were quite probably intended both for reading and dramatic presentation and may, therefore, be regarded as a facet of medieval drama.

Drama existed in medieval Spain, both in Latin and in Spanish, and, of course, in areas like Catalonia, in Catalán and its dialects, Valencian especially. Berceo might have attended a presentation in Castilian of the *Auto de los Reyes Magos (Drama of the Magi Kings)*[10] which existed in his times and formed a part of the Nativity Cycle. He might also have witnessed a play based upon the Resurrection Cycle, although not one of these has survived in Spanish.

The proverb was always popular in Spain, and is to this day. Berceo interlarded his works with homely, folksy proverbs, demonstrating his knowledge for and attraction to this form. Collections of proverbs existed in Spanish in his times, but these are of erudite backgrounds and are a far cry from Berceo's popular proverbs which stem from the rural and more humble levels of society.[11]

Berceo might well have read short stories, parables, apologues and related forms, for such stories existed. In popular lore, in chronicles, in saints' lives, in books of fables, he could have read such brief fiction. And such novelesque pieces as *Barlaam and Josephat,* the *Book of the Seven Sages* or *Book of Sindibad,*[12] though not penned in Spanish until after his time, could possibly have existed. He must have heard (or read) certain of the novels of chivalry related in his times, but not extant today in thirteenth-century versions. One, at least, the famous *Amadís de Gaula (Amadis of Gaul)* seems to have come down in its original form from Berceo's day, although the earliest extant version dates from the fifteenth century.[13]

And lastly one should always recall that for every genre of literary activity in Spanish, a similar genre in Latin was known. Berceo read Latin, and therefore, even if in the monastic libraries he utilized there was no Spanish version of the *Cantar de Mio Cid,* there may have been a Latin version, since such a version is known to have been set down. The same is true, indeed even more true, in the case of drama. Latin chronicles, sets of proverbs, Latin narrative poems, Latin lyrics (indeed the medieval Latin lyric is one of the richest of all genres and existed in all of the important countries of Western Europe) were available.[14] Quite probably most of the genres which developed in the vernaculars, provided one confines himself to literary genres and not folkloristic ones, were patterned upon Latin models. It is quite likely, then, that what Berceo read in the archives of Santo Domingo de Silos and San Millán de la Cogolla was, for the most part, written in Latin, and that all of his important works are translations or renditions of works written earlier in Latin. The vast importance of the literature of medieval Latin can hardly be overemphasized, even though for most of us today it must remain hidden.

Left until last in the discussion of literary genres or methods of literary presentation is a form of narrative verse known as the *mester de clerecía* (the school of poetry of the learned), also called *cuaderna vía* (the fourfold way) because of its arrangement in mono-rhymed quatrains. This, insofar as Gonzalo de Berceo is concerned, was the most important medium of poetic expression, since it is the medium in which almost every word of Berceo's writings is cast. Some even believe that he invented *cuaderna vía*. He is at least the first poet we know whose works appear in this medium. Much more in detail will be said about this in subsequent chapters. Let it suffice to affirm now that this poetic medium featured fourteen-syllable lines in two seven-syllable laisses or hemistichs divided by a caesura. Quatrains of full rhyme give the *mester de clerecía* a rather monotonous tone unless handled by skillful poets. In the fourteenth century another religious, the famous Juan Ruiz, Arch-priest of Hita, would utilize this poetic medium and would develop and refine it far beyond the talents of Berceo.[15]

A thirteenth-century epic-type work, the *Libro de Alexandre (Book of Alexander)*, quite aptly describes and names this poetic medium. Its author wrote:

> I use a handsome meter, it is not the minstrel's,
> It is a meter without fault, for it is of the clergy;
> It tells a rhymed tale through the fourfold way,
> In counted syllables which is a great skill.

> *(Mester traigo fermoso, non es de juglaria,*
> *mester es sin pecado ca es de clerecia,*
> *fablar curso rimado por la cuaderna via,*
> *a silabas contadas que es de gran maestria.)*[16]

The foundations of a fecund literature existed, then, when Gonzalo de Berceo penned his pious works. Upon such a foun-dation, based on Latin writings as well as Spanish, he built a sig-nificant edifice of literary production.

CHAPTER 2

Berceo Revealed in His Works

I *Berceo's Life*

EVERY literature has its anonymous or unknown writers, whose names, even when we have them, mean little today. Spain's greatest medieval literary masterpiece, the fourteenth-century *Libro de buen amor (Book of Good Love),*[1] is attributed to a Juan Ruiz, Archpriest of Hita, but no one knows whether or not such an archpriest existed or whether or not his name is a pseudonym. In spite of this, all who read the *Libro* emerge from its perusal with definite ideas about the man who penned it. Vivid and sprightly wit, deep wisdom, extreme tolerance of human failings, wry humor, love of life, and a touching sympathy for unhappy humanity are only some of the facets of the author's great soul. He who reads the *Libro de buen amor* feels that he would like to have met and known Juan Ruiz, were that possible, and feels, too, that he does know him, even though an actual meeting is impossible.

A nameless Spanish writer produced the well-known twelfth-century epic poem, the *Cantar de Mio Cid (Lay of My Cid).*[2] Less skillful and a far poorer storyteller than Homer, this unknown author even so portrays with marked empathy the eleventh-century milieu and the Cid's place in it. Who can doubt that he was a member of the Cid's armies and probably even one of the Cid's personal retinue?

Gonzalo de Berceo shares the talent of Juan Ruiz, and shares likewise almost the same degree of anonymity, so little do we know of him. Like the Spanish Chaucer, as the Archpriest of Hita has been called, Berceo establishes rapport with his reader today, even as he must have in the thirteenth century. Such talent is the true mark of greatness. How important is it, then, that we have so few vital statistics about Berceo, whose name is the first to be associated with literary works produced in Spain? It is not very important, since Berceo reveals himself as he writes far more effectively than the best of biographers might have revealed him. So does Homer reveal himself and so does the author of the *Lay of My Cid.*

Gonzalo de Berceo was not in his own century an important figure. He had none of the sophistication of a Chaucer, he did not, apparently, belong to a noble family, nor did he rise high in the hierarchy of the Benedictine Order. He did not even dwell in one of Spain's greatest monasteries. In other words, this Gonzalo, who took his surname from the village of Berceo where he was born and where the Monastery of San Millán de la Cogolla was located, insofar as can be gathered from extant records, was a simple cleric who did not leave his native region, the Province of La Rioja in New Castile. He was, however, well enough educated for his time, was practical and probably even eminently successful as a monk, and what is more pertinent to us today, he was a human being of deep faith and devotion, whose attempt to develop affinity with his public enabled him to produce a sizable body of writing, eminently Spanish in character and most representative of his century.

Scholars have been active in their perusal of monastic documents in an effort to learn about Berceo, the man. Their investigations, however, have yielded actually very little of importance. They provide little more than a simple list of ecclesiastical positions he held. A.G. Solalinde, in the prologue to his sixth edition of Berceo's *Milagros de Nuestra Señora (Miracles of Our Lady),* sums up most of what various investigators have discovered in the monastic documents in the archives of San Millán de la Cogolla which mention Berceo. These are dated 1220, 1221, and 1222. In 1221 Berceo was a deacon. Solalinde reminds his readers that in order to hold this ecclesiastical position one had to be at least twenty-three years old, leading to the supposition that Berceo was born in 1198. A document dated 1228, discovered in the cathedral archives of Calahorra, is signed by Berceo. Another document, dated 1237, also includes Berceo's signature among those of other village priests. In a Latin document, dated 1240, he is listed with other clerics. The year 1242 provides a document in which we read of him as one of the clerics of the village of Berceo, while still another, written in 1246, classifies him as a priest. Lastly, a manuscript of 1264 alludes to a will, probably dated between 1236 and 1242, in which Berceo was named as *maestre de confesión* (confessor) and as *cabezalero* (executor) of a certain Garci Gil.[3]

Brian Dutton, who has quite recently examined the archives of San Millán de la Cogolla, cites a hitherto unmentioned document of 1228 which places "don Gonzalo de Berceo en Banares" and adds to the 1240 date the name of the town of Fonzaleche in which

Berceo was a cleric. Dutton, allowing slightly more latitude than previous scholars, postulates Berceo's year of birth as either 1197 or 1198.[4] It would seem, then, that Berceo spent the greater part of his life in the Monastery of San Millán and occasionally lived as an uncloistered cleric and even as a priest in the village of Berceo.

Berceo himself tells us of his connections with San Millán and the village of Berceo:

> I, Gonzalo by name, called "of
> Berceo," educated in San Millán . . .
>
> *(Yo, Gonzalo por nombre, clamado de*
> *Verceo, de Sant Millan criado . . .)*
>   (*Santo Domingo*, Quatrain 757)

And again:

> Gonzalvo was the name of him who made this treatise,
> in Upper San Millán he was reared as a child . . .
>
> *(Gonzalvo fue so nomne que fizo est tractado,*
> *en San Millan de Suso fue de ninnez criado . . .)*
>   (*San Millán*, Quatrain 489)

Although not considered in his own time as a great writer, his works were recognized and respected. Even the Marqués de Santillana, in his famous *Prohemio y Carta al Condestable de Portugal (Introduction and Letter to the Constable of Portugal)*[5] in the fourteenth century, mentions him. Nor was Berceo unknown in the sixteenth century. Juan Hurtado de Mendoza in *El libro de buen placer (Book of Good Pleasure)* spoke of Berceo, explaining that he was a very good poet of older times who praised God with sincere devotion. The opinions of modern poets and critics will be treated later in this chapter.

There is little doubt, then, that Berceo was educated at San Millán and it is quite probable that he wore its Benedictine habit during most of his life. From San Millán he went from time to time to the Monastery of Santo Domingo de Silos where he established strong ties. Brother Alfonso Andrés, O.S.B., in his study and edition of *La Vida de Santo Domingo de Silos,* states that San Millán Monastery and Santo Domingo de Silos Monastery kept strong and cordial relationships. Berceo apparently was welcome in both and was highly esteemed. Father P. Vergara, in the Prologue to his lengthy *Vida y Milagros de el Thaumaturgo Español (Life and Miracles of Spanish Miracle Workers),* affirms that Berceo was asked by the brethren of San Millán to render into Spanish the Latin *vita* of Santo Domingo, written by Grimaldus, and that to this we owe Berceo's work on this saint.

Father Andrés believes, even though no chronicle avers it, that Berceo visited and dwelt also for some time in Santo Domingo and that he even visited San Pedro de Arlanza Monastery. Father Andrés cites lines in Berceo's work to support this statement. In quatrain 187 in the *Vida de Santo Domingo de Silos,* we read a brief description of the Castle of Carazo, near Silos:

> In the country of Carazo of which you have heard,
> A lofty fortress, a famous castle,
> There is a monastery, which was a wealthy place,
> But it was in such a plight that it was almost in ruins.

Later, in quatrain 265, Berceo writes about Arlanza:

> Over against the country of Lara, as far as the boundary,
> On the River Arlanza, in an angle of it,
> Lay a monastery, an honored house,
> San Pedro de Arlanza it is called by name.

Berceo could have heard about these monasteries, admittedly, but when one considers the following passage from *El Duelo de la Virgen,* the belief that Berceo was at Silos is strengthened. In a bas-relief in the Romanesque cloister of Silos can be seen a portrayal of Jesus' descent from the Cross. Berceo follows this with such exactitude as to preclude any doubt that he studied it carefully, possibly even writing quatrains 150–152 with the portrayal before him:

> He of Arimathea, who had claimed it [Jesus' body],
> Summoned Nichodemus, a worthy man;
> One clasps the body in his arms,
> The other drew out the hard driven nails.

> From the Lord who did nothing ever in vain
> They pulled them first from the right hand,

And it lowered him a little, and he was less heavy;
It seems to me that he was lowered all the way to the earth.

Actually, it is not until the seventeenth century that scholars became fully aware of Berceo's poems and began to investigate him and his works. Men like Tomás Antonio Sánchez in the eighteenth century and Pascual de Gayangos in the next edited his works and made them available.[6]

Earlier it was mentioned in passing that Berceo made himself known in his poems. His remarks about himself, it is true, are at best fragmentary, but nonetheless they enable his readers to understand him and to sense the kind of man he was. Out of the bits and snippets, scattered more or less unevenly and at random throughout the poems, one can piece together a pleasant and intimate portrait.

II Berceo's Rapport with His Audience

We have seen how he named himself and his place of birth. It should be pointed out also that he recognized and utilized all the homely skills of a small-town cleric to gain rapport with his rustic audiences. Close and intimate contact has always been a necessity to priests who would form strong ties with their parishioners. Such efforts had from age-old times also rewarded the various kinds of professional entertainers—*juglares* or reciters of epic and other types of narrative poetry—and of course had been utilized also by primitive bards, both secular and ecclesiastical. Folklorists[7] today know that the successful tellers of folktales or reciters of folk epics and ballads must descend to the cultural level of their audiences if they are to succeed in their trade. Berceo, therefore, went to some lengths to identify himself to his listeners and his readers as a simple member of the rural community.

He often used the first person, sometimes in the singular and sometimes in the plural. And even though he does not always give his name, he makes it quite obvious that it is he who is speaking. A few examples will suffice:

I wish to write a poem in polished Romance;

(Quiero fer una prosa en roman paladino;)
(Santo Domingo, 2)

I wish to climb for a bit in these trees.

(Quiero en estas arbores un ratiello sobir.)
(Milagros, 45)

and

In his honor I should like to prepare a writing,

(En su honor querria fer una escriptura,)
(Sacrificio de la Misa, 1)

Such use of the first person had strong appeal and established firm rapport when poets recited before groups of listeners, and to a lesser extent when people read works aloud in the first person.

Sometimes Berceo casually makes a reference to some everyday kind of activity and associates it with himself:

There were some steps and stairs in the column:
We are accustomed to see such in carven towers;
I have climbed some of these quite often.

(Avia la coluna escalones e gradas:
Veer solemos tales en las torres obradas:
Yo sobi por algunas, esto muchas vegadas.)
(Santa Oria, 39)

Berceo seems to have written for audiences who would listen to rather than read his poems. Such people, Berceo well knew, could quickly allow their interest to flag. The catching of attention, and even more the task of maintaining it, therefore, was of great importance to him. Hence his repeated references to his own feelings. At one place he speaks of his own personal weariness which must be overcome:

I wish in my old age, although I am weary,
To write about this holy virgin in Spanish.

(Quiero en mi vegez, maguer so ya cansado,
De esta sancta virgen romanzar su dictado.)
(Santa Oria, 2)

He even uses the technique of calling himself a sinner, like his fellowman, so as to place himself on his audiences' level:

For me, who above others sinned, I beg grace.
Turn to me, Mother, do not cast me into oblivion;
Take me from where I lie mired in sin;
I am a captive in Egypt, sins have betrayed me.

(Por mi, que sobre todos peque, merced te pido.
Torna sobre me, Madre, non me eches en olvido;
Trayme del peccado do yago embebido;
Preso so en Egipto, los vicios me an vendido.)
(*Loores de Nuestra Señora,* 231)

Once, at least, borrowing from the manner of oral presentation
of the troubadours and *juglares,* he injects himself directly into the
minds of his audience by asking for a reward for his verses which
he had written for the common people and not in Latin. "It would
indeed be worth, as I believe, a glass of good wine," he wrote in
La Vida de Santo Domingo de Silos, quatrain 2. The reference to
the payment in wine for good entertainment he may have borrowed
from the *juglares* who performed for money. If Berceo could win
for his beloved monasteries donations from parishioners who
seemed reluctant to come forward, he need not be condemned. If
some of his works were written to convince people that certain
donations were owed the monasteries, as Brian Dutton[8] has shown
to be a strong possibility, he was doing only what more self-centered
poets were doing less enviably to line their own purses. But no
matter what his reason or reasons, the end products, the works
themselves, are what count and not their *raison d'être.*

We have seen how Berceo attempted to make his audiences see
him as a member of their own milieu when he told them that he
was from Berceo and of their own region. This personal touch,
this effort to appear as a man cut from the same cloth as his fol-
lowers, is found in all his works. Each occurrence of an allusion to
himself has been collected and set down in Joaquín Artiles' recent
study, and no less than seven such passages mention Gonzalo de
Berceo by name.[9]

Still another approach used by Berceo to establish affinity with
his public must now be treated, because to my knowledge it has
received only the briefest of allusions and because it is important.
This is the use of coarse and even gross descriptions and details
which Berceo evidently believed would attract the attention of
those who read or heard his works read. The poet knew his audience
for what is was—a roughhewn and earthy populace, crude and

coarse and primitive. Noble as well as commoner shared these characteristics, nor were such tastes confined to the masculine part of the population.

This kind of writing, which went back to Classical Antiquity, was one of the several styles of literary activity recognized by the literati. It was known as "low style," as opposed to the purer and more edifying styles. Berceo did not indulge in "low style" in all of his works, although his previously mentioned proclivities for colloquial usages and grammar and homely images would have relegated his works, in the minds of some of his contemporaries, to that category. "Low style" appeals to the coarser fibers of the human psyche. It is, of course, present today in works often termed "realistic," and it has been a part of the literatures of all cultures in all periods.

Curtius has pointed out that the literature of "low style" is not necessarily a literature of realism, but not even his erudite pronouncement can effectively and completely divorce vulgarity, coarse words, and gross concepts and the attributes of "low style" from what we consider to be realism.

Most medieval authors, but not all, felt no embarrassment before coarseness and obscenity. Consider Chaucer's *The Miller's Tale* in all its titillating grossness and utter obscenity, or Juan Ruiz's rough and lewd wit as he describes certain of the "mountain maidens," or consider especially some of the vilest of the *fabliaux,* and one begins to understand the complete freedom with which medieval authors treated their subject matter. The language of the barracks did not offend them, and even courtly gentlemen like Chaucer and Alfonso the Wise employed the "low style."

Berceo employed it, too, but he did not do so to cater primarily to the baser appetites or to provoke rough laughter. When he brought coarse concepts into his works, it was primarily to drive home, by descending to his public's level, the lesson of the preachments he was making in his narrations; but—and this is an important facet of his technique—he walked a thin line between serious preachment and humor. The grossest and frankest of all his miracles, number VIII, generally entitled *El Romero de Santiago (St. James's Pilgrim),* exemplifies this perfectly.

Berceo relates the story, reminding his reader that it was taken from the works of St. Hugo of Cluny. A friar who habitually sinned carnally decided to go on a pilgrimage to St. James's tomb at

Compostela. Unable to stifle his lust, he had intercourse with his mistress the night before he started for Compostela. We read in quatrain 185:

> When he was about to depart, he committed a sin:
> Instead of his vigil he lay with his woman,
> And he sought no penance as the faith demands,
> And took the road with his wicked harvest.

> *(Quando a essir ovieron, fizo una nemiga:*
> *En logar de vigilia iogó con su amiga,*
> *Non tomó penitençia commo la ley prediga,*
> *Metiose al camino con su mala hortiga.)*

On the road the devil met him, disguised as St. James, and exacted a fearful penance, of which we read in quatrain 192:

> The false St. James said: "This is the judgment:
> That you cut off the members which committed fornication;
> As soon as you cut them off, you will do God a service,
> Since with your flesh itself you will render sacrifice to Him."

> *(Disso el falso Iacob: esti es el iudiçio:*
> *Que te cortes los miembros que façen el forniçio,*
> *Dessent que te deguelles, farás a Dios serviçio,*
> *Que de tu carne misma li farás sacrifiçio.)*

The poor friar believed the devil, castrated himself, and bled to death. With something close to relish Berceo writes of the devil's triumph, injecting wry humor into his account in quatrain 197:

> He who gave this advice, together with his attendants,
> The large and the small, the lesser and the greater,
> All the false traitors seized upon his soul,
> Bearing it to the flames and to horrid sweatings.

> *(El que dió el conseio con sus atenedores,*
> *Los grandes e los chicos, menudos e maiores,*
> *Trabaron de la alma los falsos traydores,*
> *Levabanla al fuego a los malos suores.)*

St. James quickly came to the rescue of the friar's soul, but the devils argued, and the Saint sought the judgment of the Virgin Mary. She ruled in favor of St. James, restored the friar to life, but minus the offending sexual organs which had led to his death. The two quatrains (all of 212 and part of 213) which describe his cure are gross in the extreme, and yet in keeping with the period and with the tastes and sentiments of the medieval audience:

> He was in all else sound and cured,
> Save for a small scar which he had upon him;
> But as to the genitals as much as were cut off,
> Not a portion grew back, they were completely absent.

> He was quite healed, entirely sound, although
> A little hole remained so that he could make water;
> He assessed the parts which he had lost,
> He planned to go his way happy and satisfied.

> *(Era de lo al todo sano e meiorado,*
> *Fuera de un filiello que tenie travesado;*
> *Mas lo de la natura quanto que fo cortado,*
> *Non li creçió un punto, fincó en su estado.*

> *De todo era sano, todo bien encorado,*
> *Pora verter su agua fincoli el forado,*
> *Requirió su repuesto lo que traie trossado,*
> *Pensó de ir su via alegre e pagado.)*

Moreover, when he reached the end of his pilgrimage, people "witnessed the miracle," which goes beyond implication and virtually states that they verified visually what the friar told them. Read quatrain 215:

> This great miracle was proclaimed in Compostela,
> With all the people of the town coming to witness it.
> They said: "this thing we should put in writing,
> For it will delight those who in the future will hear it."

> *(Sonó por Compostela esta grant marabilla,*
> *Vinienlo a veer todos los de la villa:*
> *Diçien: esta tal cosa debriemos escribilla,*
> *Los que son por venir plazralis de oilla.)*

Berceo's narratives of these facts were not to him or to his audience in any way vulgar or tasteless. It is no more than the good cleric's straightforward and graphic account of what took place. Its "realism" set down in the "low style" handed down from antiquity was effective. Nonetheless, as people shuddered at the con-

cept of self-castration and were moved to awe at the miraculous
power of Our Lady, they must have been amused at the wording of
the story as it was handled by Berceo.

Described in Chapter 4, but in less detail, is Miracle XXI, *La
Abadesa Encinta (The Pregnant Abbess)*. The theme itself is one
calculated to attract attention. Abbesses were, of course, important
personages in the Middle Ages, powerful even secularly, and exceedingly powerful in ecclesiastical circles. That such a person as an
abbess could become pregnant was the apogee of scandal. Berceo
could not have related a more shocking event. He does not stress
the sexual overtones of the tale, but neither does he minimize these
facets. In the telling the brutally graphic description of events is
justified. The reader or hearer is drawn forcefully into the abbess's
plight and made to sympathize with her terrible dilemma, so that
Berceo can, at least in the realm of narrative technique, be excused
for an account skillfully, if very realistically, handled. The reader
immediately is attracted to the abbess, whose sin is very human
after all. The poet, almost from the first lines, hints at his own
sympathy, making it plain that forgiveness will come when peni-
tence is present:

> If people sin and make their penance well,
> God straightway pardons them for all evil-doing.
> They have from Jesus Christ all his sympathy:
> I should like to give about this a good account.

> *(Si pecaban los omnes, façien bien penitençia,*
> *Perdonabalis luego Dios toda la malquerençia,*
> *Avien con Jesu Xpo toda su atenençia:*
> *Quierovos dar a esto una buena sentençia.)*
>   (Quatrain 504)

The abbess was famous for good works and piety; however
quatrain 507 reveals her frailty:

> But the abbess at one time faltered,
> She did a crazy thing which is forbidden;
> By chance she trod upon a noxious weed;
> When once she realized it, she discovered she was pregnant.

> *(Pero la abbadesa cadió una vegada,*
> *Fizo una locura que es mucho vedada,*

Pisó por su ventura yerba fuert enconada,
Quando bien se catído, fallóse embargada.)

The nuns, whom she had often disciplined, though not unjustly, reported her to the bishop, who sent his examiner to investigate the case. The abbess threw herself down before the Virgin's image and implored first her forgiveness and then her protection. Her reply came forthwith and she was delivered painlessly of her illegitimate baby. When the bishop's judges arrived, the abbess had to endure a close physical examination, however:

> He sent his clerics in whom he trusted most,
> So that they could examine how the matter was;
> They stripped off her habit, although it embarrassed her;
> They found her so dry that she was like a board.

> They discovered in her no sign of pregnancy,
> Neither milk nor trace of blood;
> They said: "this is all nothing but a fantasy,
> Never was such a false report bandied about."

> *(Envió de sus clerigos en qui él mas fiaba,*
> *Que probassen la cosa de qual guisa estaba:*
> *Tollieronli la saia maguer que li pesaba,*
> *Fallaronla tan secca que tabla semeiaba.*

> *Non trovaron en ella signo de prennedat,*
> *Nin leche nin batuda de nulla malveztat:*
> *Dissieron: non es esto fuera grant vanidat,*
> *Nunqua fo levantada tan fiera falsedat.)*
> (Quatrains 555–556)

Berceo used details, then, effectively, if somewhat tastelessly, at least by modern standards. Two last examples will stress the point:

> She felt herself with her hands, when she was conscious,
> Her belly, her sides, and each of her flanks;
> She found her womb flat, her waist slender,
> Like a woman who is relieved of such a burden.

> *(Palpóse con sus manos quando fo recordada,*
> *Por ventre, por costados, e por cada ijada:*

Trobó so vientre llaçio, la çinta muy delgada,
Commo muger que es de tal cosa librada.)
                              (Quatrain 537)

And in quatrain 539:

> When this poor pregnant one realized she was free,
> Since the sack was emptied of its bad flour,
> She began with great joy to sing the *Salve Regina,*
> Which is the solace and the balm of those in travail.

> *(Quando se sintió libre la prennada mesquina,*
> *Fo el saco vaçio de la mala farina,*
> *Empezó con grant gozo cantar Salve Regina,*
> *Que es de los cuitados solaz e mediçina.)*

In all, Berceo included among his *Milagros de Nuestra Señora* four stories about sexual sin: numbers 2, 7, 8, and 21. In each the frankness and graphic quality of his language is notable. This matter has not been discussed at any length in previous studies of Berceo. In these modern times it seems not only permissible but even necessary to bring them to the students' attention. Along with homely and colloquial language, the poet's personal involvement in his accounts, in his efforts to build for himself in his reader's eye the image of a simple, pious and not well-educated priest, he took full advantage of the most uninhibited portrayals of the physical results of pregnancy, self-mutilation, and sexual indulgence. In doing so he was not alone, for such was the custom of the age. Indeed, Berceo was more conventional than many writers, for his detailed accounts were not written primarily to elicit mirth, but rather to reveal the charity of Our Lady toward the greatest of sinners (the suicidal friar) and toward a poor abbess who "at one time faltered."

Berceo availed himself of this means of rapport, either descending to the level of his audience deliberately, or writing as a member of his audience's stratum because he belonged to that stratum. He wrote so because it pleased him to write so, and because he believed he could appeal more strongly to his public if he made it feel at home with him.

III Cuaderna Vía *and Its Appeal*

Berceo's favorite poetic meter must in itself have been attractive to his public. We can assume, I believe, that it had popular appeal and was successful, for otherwise surely he would not have written all his works in *cuaderna vía* during many years of his life. Had he discovered that this verse form was badly received, he would surely have turned to some other form, since others had been tried and accepted. No innovator—and to some considerable extent he was an innovator in the use of *cuaderna vía* and may have been its inventor—would subject his audience to a poetic medium unpleasing or irritating or boring to that audience. Since in all probability Berceo read his works aloud to groups of illiterate people, he would quickly have detected any lack of enthusiasm, would have changed his poetic style and would not have penned thousands of lines in a medium unpleasant to his public.

Cuaderna vía was not to the medieval audience, whether literate or illiterate, a poetic medium dull, disagreeably monotonous, singsong, or otherwise without poetic quality. Indeed, Berceo's *cuaderna vía,* and of course the even more skillful *cuaderna vía* of the Archpriest of Hita in the fourteenth century, must have been heard with delight and can be read with delight today. Were this not so, the two poets who strove most actively to attract the people's interest and affection would not, could not, have composed their thousands of lines in this medium. The same can be said of Chaucer, whose *Canterbury Tales* could not have been monotonous in their own meter to that poet's contemporaries and are not monotonous to the literary today.

Proof of enthusiasm for Berceo in our own times can be found in the writings of some of the most accomplished of modern poets. Rubén Darío himself (1867–1916), that sweet singer, included in his *Prosas profanas (Profane Verses)* a warm and loving poem, "A Maestre Gonzalo de Berceo." It merits inclusion here in the original and in translation, for it makes Berceo and his poetry emerge sparkling alive and nostalgically bedewed with some of that poet's own humanity and tenderness:

To Master Gonzalo de Berceo

I love your delicious Alexandrines,
The soul of Spain, like that of Hugo;

The latter is worth a goblet of champagne,
Just as the former's a "glass of good wine."

But to either bird divine
Is the ancient prison alien;
The iron bar abuses, the shackles rasp;
Flight and freedom are their destiny.

Thus I strive to bring to life
Your antique verse whose wings I gild
And make to shine with my modern enamel;
Liberty it has with integrity,
And it comes back like the gerfalcon to the hand,
Bearing from the blue its golden rhymes.

(Amo tu delicioso alejandrino
como el de Hugo, espíritu de España;
éste vale una copa de champaña,
como aquél vale un "vaso de bon vino."

Mas a uno y otro pájaro divino
la primitiva cárcel es extraña,
el barrote maltrata, el grillo daña;
que vuelo y libertad son su destino.

Así procuro que en la luz resalte
tu antiguo verso, cuyas alas doro
y hago brillar con mi moderno esmalte;
tiene la libertad con el decoro
y vuelve como al puño el gerifalte,
trayendo del azul rimas de oro.)

Don Manuel Machado (1874–1947) composed his poem to
Berceo in the *cuaderna vía* itself and entitled it "Retablo (Altarpiece")".
Printed in his *Alma, Museo, Los Cantares (Soul, Museum, Songs)*,
it reads:

Now they both stand at the Beloved Father's right,
The two saintly men, the choir master and the besung,
The Great St. Dominic of Silos so venerated,
And the Master Gonzalo called "of Berceo."
I behold the Saint as in the poem
Written in the name of Christ and of the Glorious Virgin:
The waxen hue, the weary pilgrimage,
The loosened locks, the forehead luminous . . .

And at his side the poet, that wondrous pilgrim,
Smiles at us moderns who follow the path,
And shows us the reward of his clear destiny:
A heavenly palm-bough and a glass of good wine.

(Ya están ambos a diestra del Padre deseado,
los dos santos varones, el chantre y el cantado,
el Grant Santo Domingo de Silos venerado
y el Maestre Gonzalo de Berceo nomnado.
Yo veo al Santo como en la sabida prosa
fecha en nombre de Christo y de la Gloriosa:
la color amariella, la marcha fatigosa,
el cabello tirado, la frente luminosa . . .
Y a su lado el poeta, romero peregrino,
sonríe a los de ahora que andamos el camino,
y el galardón nos muestra de su claro destino:
una palma de gloria y un vaso de buen vino.)

Don Manuel's brother, Don Antonio Machado (1875–1939), in
his *Poesías completas (Complete Poetic Works)* included in honor
of Berceo a piece entitled "Mis poetas" ("My Poets"). It depicts
Berceo's work in darker hues, evoking less attractive vistas of the
medieval landscape and spirit.

My Poets

The first is called Gonzalo de Berceo,
Gonzalo de Berceo, poet and pilgrim,
Who on pilgrimage stumbled upon a meadow,
Whom the scholars depict copying a parchment.
He composed to St. Dominic, he composed for St. Mary,
And to St. Millán, to St. Lawrence and St. Oria.
And he said: "my poem is not in the minstrels' style;
We have it written; it is a true account."
His verse is sweet and serious, repetitive files
Of wintry poplar trees, in which naught glistens;
Lines like furrows in dusky plowed land,
And in the distance the azure mountains of Castile.
He tells us of the solace of the weary pilgrim;
Reading in saints' lives and books of prayer,
Copying ancient histories, he tells us his account
Whilst the glow of his spirit makes its way to view.

(El primero es Gonzalo de Berceo llamado,
Gonzalo de Berceo, poeta y peregrino,

> que yendo en romería acaeció en un prado,
> y a quien los sabios pintan copiando un pergamino.
> Trovó a Santo Domingo, trovó a Santa María,
> y a San Millán, y a San Lorenzo y Santa Oria.
> Y dijo: mi dictado non es de juglaría;
> escrito lo tenemos; es verdadera historia.
> Su verso es dulce y grave; monótonas hileras
> de chopos invernales, en donde nada brilla;
> renglones como surcos en pardas sementeras,
> y lejos, las montañas azules de Castilla.
> El nos cuenta el repaire del romeo cansado;
> leyendo en santorales y libros de oración,
> copiando historias viejas, nos dice su dictado,
> mientras le sale afuera la luz del corazón.)

And Enrique de Mesa, in his *Cancionero Castellano (Castilian Song Book)*, waxes ecstatic at the end of his poem entitled "El bon vino" ("The Good Wine"):

> To continue my journey
> And to forget desire
> Oh Gonzalo de Berceo!
> The good wine!
>
> *(Para seguir mi camino*
> *también olvidar deseo.*
> *¡Oh Gonzalo de Berceo!*
> *¡El bon vino!)*

The full rhyme of *cuaderna vía*'s quatrains has power. It catches the reader in its net and carries him along with force and sometimes with violence. Once entrapped, once caught up in the metrics and trained to march to the regular and unchanging cadence, once taught to expect each line in each quatrain to rhyme completely with each of the other lines, the reader surrenders to *cuaderna vía*'s spell and reads on tirelessly. Poets from time immemorial have learned to take advantage of what some regard as monotony, of what others prefer to regard as an acceptable and often as a vigorous flow and modulation. The *Kalevala*, Finland's national epos, written in eight-syllabled trochaic verse, partakes of somewhat the same monotony unjustly ascribed to *cuaderna vía*. A folk epic, composed for a rude and untutored people, this work had to attract and compel attention. Its composers understood the power of repetition and its tonal beat. A good idea of the *Kalevala*'s style and versification can be obtained from Longfellow's *Hiawatha*, which is a pretty true imitation of it:

> Bright before it beat the water,
> Beat the clear and sunny water,
> Beat the shining Big-Sea-Water,
> etc.

The *Iliad* and the *Odyssey,* undying poems, varied little as they related in the unchanging six-footed measures of hexameter some of literature's greatest moments. No one saw monotony in the *Iliad* or the *Odyssey*. Of course hexameter's sameness lay in cadence rather than in rhyme, whereas in Berceo's medium both cadence and rhyme are repeated.

Latin hexameters, for example those utilized by Virgil in his *Aeneid,* can illustrate repetitive quality of ancient epics:
Ārmă vĭ/rūmquĕ că/nō Trō/iaĕ quī/prīmŭs ăb/ōris.

Longfellow, to use this poet again as an example, wrote a form of hexameter, substituting accent for the quantity of the ancient epics. In *Evangeline* we find

> This is the forest primeval. The murmuring pines
>   and the hemlocks,
> Bearded with moss, and in garments green, indistinct
>   in the twilight,
> Stand like Druids of eld, with voices sad and
>   prophetic,
> Stand like harpers hoar, with beards that rest on
>   their bosoms.

Monotony? Perhaps to some, but to nineteenth-century literate America definitely not.

And so Berceo, viewed by his contemporaries, no doubt seemed attractive. Continuance, flow, a kind of marching forward along a definite poetic path marked carefully by counted syllables, a definite break after the seventh, and full rhyme at the end of each line captured and moved the Bercean audience. Whether one chooses a narrative passage:

No matter that the fire was so strong and so hot,
It did not reach the lady nor did it reach the child,
Nor did it reach the curtain which hung before them,
Nor did it do a penny's worth of damage.

(Maguer que fué el fuego tan fuert e tan quemant,
Nin plegó a la duenna, nin plegó al ifant,
Nin plegó al flabello que colgava delant,
Ni li fizo de danno un dinero pesant.)

(*Milagros,* quatrain 324)

or a descriptive passage:

All wore chasubles of brilliant colors,
Crosiers in their left hands like preachers,
Chalices of the best gold in their right hands,
They appeared as ministers of a wondrous master.

(Todos vestian casullas de preçiosos colores,
Blagos en las siniestras comme predicadores,
Caliçes en las diestras de oro muy meiores,
Semeiaba ministros de preçiosos sennores.)

(*Santa Oria,* quatrain 58)

or a passage of didactic or instructional nature:

It is fitting that we examine this holy mystery,
No little task is it to scrutinize it,
But He who guided David in the psalter,
Will give us counsel for this goal.

(Conviene que catemos est sancto misterio,
En bien escodrinarlo non es poco lazerio,
Mas el que a David guió en est sallerio,
El nos dara conseio a est desiderio.)

(*Sacrificio,* quatrain 241)

or a passage designed to exalt or glorify:

Blessed Lady, gifted Queen,
Crowned by the hand of thy Son, Sir Christ,
Free us from the minions of the devil,
Who always maintains an evil siege against our souls.

(Sennora benedicta, Reina acabada,
Por mano del tu fijo don Christo coronada,

> *Libranos del diablo de la su çancaiada,*
> *Que tiene a las almas siempre mala celada.)*
> (*Milagros,* quatrain 910)

In no matter what context the poet guides his audience along a path so well marked and, indeed, so walled in, there is no escape until the poem ends.

Cuaderna vía, the fourfold way used by clerics like Berceo and Juan Ruiz a century after him, or by those who composed lengthy secular narratives like the *Libro de Apolonio,* was a successful and effective poetic medium for all varieties of subject matter.

As the individual works of Berceo are treated in chapters devoted to each of these, more of Berceo's techniques will be studied. What has been set down so far has been intended to orient the reader in a general way and to prepare him for later detailed treatment. More careful examination of the several works or classes of work will reveal that Gonzalo de Berceo may have been motivated by a number of influences when he penned his poems—reasons purely devout, reasons devout and at the same time didactic, and still others devout and also propagandistic.

With this brief sketch of his life and of his place in society, the reader is turned back upon himself and must for himself create an image of Gonzalo de Berceo the man. The titles of works attributed to Berceo, each to be treated at length in the chapters that follow, are listed below. To the left are labels that categorize the three areas of subject matter covered by the poems:

The Virgin *Milagros de Nuestra Señora (Miracles of Our Lady)*

Lives of Saints *Vida de Santo Domingo de Silos (Life of St. Dominic of Silos)*

Vida de San Millán de La Cogolla (Life of St. Aemilianus of La Cogolla)

Vida de Santa Oria (Life of St. Aurea)

Martirio de San Lorenzo (Martyrdom of St. Lawrence)

Doctrinal Poems *Duelo que Fizo la Virgin (The Lament Which the Virgin Made)*

Loores de Nuestra Señora (Praises of the Virgin)

El Sacrificio de la Misa (Sacrifice of the Mass)

De los Signos que Aparescerán ante el Juicio (Of the Signs Which Will Appear Before Judgment Day)

Hymnos (Hymns)

CHAPTER 3

The Milagros de Nuestra Señora

THE *Milagros de Nuestra Señora (Miracles of Our Lady)*[1] represents Berceo's most inspired verses and with good reason. The Blessed Virgin, who appears as a character in the twenty-five miracles, was in the Middle Ages the most beloved of divine figures, the most accessible to mortals, the favorite protagonist of religious writings. Old and young, rich and poor, healthy and sick, all looked to her for protection, solace, or healing. In literature people of all professions called upon her: soldiers and sailors survived battle and shipwreck through her intervention; captives escaped their dungeons through her help; farmers and city dwellers depended upon her clemency; housewives and prostitutes, Christians, and occasionally deserving Jews and Moors sought her aid; the clergy in all levels of the hierarchy expected her protection; even animals benefited from her mercy. In Berceo's time the worship of Mary—Mary the Mother, for it was true worship—assumed such proportions among clergy and laity as to eclipse the worship of the Father and the Son. Her shrines, some magnificent, some humble, increased in number across the Iberian Peninsula, as well as throughout the rest of Christian Europe. Some of these shrines attracted an international clientele of pilgrims who came from far away to honor her at Saragossa, Montserrat, and Guadalupe. Other shrines were of local fame only and attracted hunters, farmers, and fishermen from remote rural districts. Still others were constructed in the back streets and alleys of the smaller towns and villages and in the slums of cities. Even the names of many no longer exist.[2]

But art survives to prove the Virgin's importance in medieval culture: paintings, miniatures, and frescoes depicted her miracles; musicians composed countless songs of praise to her; cathedrals and lowly parish churches alike proudly displayed sculptured friezes and fondly-chiselled images of her.[3] And the literature of the Church, whether couched in Latin or in the vernaculars, was richer for her part in it. No less rich in her lore and her miracles was the unwritten literature of the folk.[4]

It is difficult today to comprehend the greatness of the role of
the Virgin Mary in the medieval world. And yet, if one pauses to
think for a moment, her importance in life and literature today
still remains and makes its impact. Thousands still visit Lourdes,
Fatima, and Montserrat. The Church of Our Lady of Guadalupe
in Mexico City still attracts endless lines of the faithful. In shrines
of local vintage, too, votive candles still flicker before her images.
And to this day new miracles are attributed to her even in lands as
skeptical and iconoclastic as our own.

I Sources of Berceo's Miracles

Since in thirteenth-century Spain Mariolatry and Mariology
reached a crest, it is understandable that a devout parish priest
like Gonzalo de Berceo should prepare an anthology of Mary-
miracles and should present it in the distinctly reverent human way
he chose to present it. His efforts, of course, had many precedents
in pious writings in Latin and some, even, in the vernaculars. Famous by Berceo's time were certain collections of miracles of the
Virgin, and such in all probability had come to his attention. Copies
of Gautier de Coincy's Miracles de la Sainte Vièrge (Miracles of
the Holy Virgin) set down in Medieval French a century before
Berceo's Milagros, could well have been carried into Spain in the
original or in translation; Vincent of Beauvais' Latin Speculum
Historiale (Mirror of History) was known later in the century to
have been sent to King Alfonso X, and might quite probably have
appeared even earlier in Spanish monasteries, as might have appeared also the well-known and widely disseminated De Miraculis Beatae Mariae Virginis (Of the Miracles of the Blessed Virgin
Mary). Walter of Cluny's De Miraculis Beatae Mariae (Of the
Miracles of the Blessed Virgin Mary), the Scala Coeli (Ladder of
Heaven), Johannes Gobius Junior's Liber Miraculis Sanctae
Mariae Dei Genetricis (The Book of the Miracles of St. Mary the
Mother of God), Mariale Magnum (Greatness of Mary) which
was attributed without authority to Spain's St. Isidore of Seville,
and the Liber Mariae (Book of Mary) of Gil Zamora, Berceo's
contemporary, might well have been accessible to Berceo.

But even without such well-known collections of miracles probably available to him, Berceo would have been able to produce his
Milagros. He simply made use of a particular Latin collection,

possibly well known, and certainly extant in his time.[5] This collection had been assembled by some nameless author who had drawn upon several of the famous collections mentioned above, notably from the miracles found in the works of Vincent of Beauvais, Gautier de Coincy, and Jacobus de Voragine. Berceo took this collection, and, using it as his primary source, rewrote its miracles in Spanish verse, producing a book far more readable than the Latin original. This is the *Milagros de Nuestra Señora.* Although he followed the content of the Latin collection even to the degree of presenting the miracles in Spanish in exactly the same order as the Latin, he managed to attain remarkable originality.[6] Where the Latin, as we have it, set forth the events in a stark and undecorated prose, Berceo utilized the poetic medium, the *cuaderna vía,* to be discussed again in detail subsequently, thereby giving a new and happier mode of presentation. Moreover, he imparted to his verses a particularly personal tone, with touches of local color, rustic Spanish speech, and proverbial expressions, delightfully phrased in a manner designed to allow Berceo himself to introduce each miracle. His personal touch is everpresent.

Perhaps it would be valuable to present a few passages from the Latin collection utilized by Berceo, with Berceo's own rendition into Spanish and each with its translation into English. The reader will grasp immediately the vast difference between the Latin original and the Spanish of Berceo. How much more expressive, how much more detailed, and how much more colorful and lively is Berceo's treatment than that of his source!

No matter where one chooses to make a comparison between the Latin and the Spanish rendition of it, he finds that Berceo develops surprising tones of originality. Berceo is no mere translator, as some have averred, but actually a skilled poet who reads his source knowledgeably, and then writes its content in his own words, shifting from the bare prose account of the Latin into a polished poetic version. No one can translate from prose into a strictly poetic formula like the *cuaderna vía* and expect to be literal, of course, for the demands of versification inevitably force the poet to give parallel but not exact meanings and may, indeed, compel him to wander from the exact meaning of his source. Berceo encountered these difficulties, but was not disturbed by them.

Let us take lines from the first miracle, which has been given the title of "La Casulla de San Ildefonso" ("Saint Ildefonso's Chas-

uble"). The first few verses of Berceo's Spanish, when compared
with the Latin source he used, reveals much:

> *Fuit in toletana urbe quidam*
> *archiepiscopus qui vocabatur*
> *hildefonsus, religiosus valde*
> *et bonis operibus ornatus;*

> *qui inter cetera bonorum operum*
> *studia sanctam dei genitricem*
> *mariam multum diligebat et, prout*
> *poterat, omni reverencia eam*
> *honorabat.*

(There was in the Toledan city a certain
archbishop who was called Hildefonsus, a
clergyman accomplished in good works;
who among other studies of good works
greatly loved St. Mary, the Mother of God, and
insofar as he was able, honored her
with all reverence.)

> *En Toledo la buena, essa villa real*
> *Que iaze sobre Taio, essa agua cabdal,*
> *Ovo un arzobispo, coronado leal,*
> *Que fue de la Gloriosa amigo natural.*

> *Dizienli Yldefonso, dizlo la escriptura,*
> *Pastor que a su grei dava buena pastura:*
> *Omne de sancta vida que trásco grand cordura:*
> *Que nos mucho digamos so fecho lo mestura.*

> *Siempre con la Gloriosa ovo su atenencia,*
> *Nunqua varon en duenna metió major querencia,*
> *En buscarli servicio methie toda femencia,*
> *Facie en ello seso e buena providencia.*
>
>   (Quatrains 48–50)

(In fair Toledo, that royal city that lies above the Tajo's mighty flood,
there lived an archbishop, a faultless cleric, and he was a consummate
devotee of the Glorious Virgin. His name was Ildefonso according to the
records, and he was a shepherd who provided good pasturage for his
flock. He was a man of pious life, possessing great prudence, and since
his deeds reveal all this, it is meet that we declare it. To the Glorious Virgin
he was ever attentive, and no man ever loved a lady more. To serving her

he directed all his zeal, and he did this with wisdom and with forethought.)
(This translation comes from *Medieval Age* in Dell's *Laurel Masterpieces of World Literature*)

We see Toledo described in eulogistic terms as "the fair," while the Latin avoided even the proper name and used the adjectival "Toledan" city. Also Berceo names the River Tajo, eulogizing it as "that mighty flood," although he found no mention at all of the river in the Latin text. Berceo describes Ildefonso as "a consummate devotee of the Glorious Virgin" and as a "faultless cleric." The Latin source merely mentions that he is "worthy and ornate in good works," with no reference to his sentiments about the Virgin. Ildefonso is described by Berceo as "a shepherd who provided good pasturage for his flock," with the statement about his pious life and great prudence.

In essence, then, the Latin prose is concise and simple and even stark and bare, while the Spanish is enriched by its poetic presentation, colorfully descriptive passages, formulistic phraseology, the personalization of Ildefonso, and the eulogistic references to Toledo and the Tajo. The reader, or hearer, moreover, is led to associate the poet with his creation, for frequently he used the first person plural to establish rapport between himself and his audience in such passages as *Que nos mucho digamos* (it is meet that we declare it).

Occasionally Berceo goes so far, then, as to set down phrases and sentences, indeed entire concepts and ideas not found in the Latin at all. Take the following sequence, for example, surely one of the most vivid in the way of contrast in proof of Berceo's originality:

> *Ille vero cu-*
> *piens alcius eam honorare consti-*
> *tuit, ut celebraretur sollempnitas*
> *eius singulis annis octavo die*
>
> *ante festivitatem dominici na-*
> *talis, ut ita videlicet, si*
> *sollempnitas annunciacionis do-*
> *minice circa passionem vel re-*
>
> *surreccionem domini evenerit,*
> *in predicto die sub eadem*

sollempnitate congrue restitui
possit. Quod sibi satis vide-

batur iustum, ut prius sancte
dei genitricis ageretur festum,
ex qua deus homo natus venit
in mundum.

(He, however, desiring to honor Mary in a more exalted way, decreed
that she be celebrated each year on the eighth day before the festival of
the Lord's birthday, in order thereby that if the celebration of the Lord's
Annunciation should occur near the Passion or Resurrection season, it
could be rescheduled on the designated day to coincide with that earlier
celebration. It seemed proper to him that the festival of the Holy Mother
of God should be held first, since it was she from whom God incarnate
came into the world.)

> *Fizol otro servicio el leal coronado,*
> *Fizoli una fiesta en decienbre mediado,*
> *La que cae en marzo dia mui sennalado*
> *Quando Gabriel vino con el rico mandado.*
>
> *Quando Grabriel vino con la messaleria,*
> *Quando sabrosamientre dixo: "Ave Maria,"*
> *E dissoli por nueva que pariria a Messia*
> *Estando tan entrega como era al dia.*
>
> *Estonz cae un tiempo, esto por connocia,*
> *Non canta la Eglesia canto de alegria,*
> *Non lieva so derecho tan sennalado dia;*
> *Si bien lo comedieremos fizo grand cortesia.*
>
> *Fizo grand providencia el amigo leal,*
> *Que puso essa festa cerca de la natal,*
> *Asento buena vinna cerca de buen parral,*
> *La madre con el Fijo, par que no e egual.*

(Quatrains 52–55)

(The loyal tonsured one celebrated in the middle of December a festival
of hers that formerly fell in March upon the momentous day when Gabriel
came with the priceless message, when he with rapture cried "Hail Mary!"
and gave her the news that she, a virgin, would bear the Messiah. In that
other season the Church sings no songs of joy, nor does such an outstanding
day receive its due. If one gives the matter careful thought, he did a great
service.

The faithful devotee made, therefore, an important decree, for he set
this feast day close to Christmas, thus planting a noble vine close to a fine
arbor, the Mother with the Son, a pair with no equal.)

One last passage, taken from the end of the miracle, should be added to this brief study of Berceo's ability to rise above the Latin source's threadbare account. As above, we give first the Latin, then Berceo's interpretation of the passage:

> *Sic sancta dei genitrix*
> *beatum Hyldefonsum, qui ei*
> *devote servierat, honoravit.*
> *Siagrii vero presumpcionem*
> *morte multavit ostendens*
> *quia, quisquis eam honoraverit,*
> *graciam dei et suam habebit.*

(And so the holy mother of God honored the blessed Hyldefonsus, who had devoutly served her. And yet she punished with death the arrogance of Siagrius, revealing that whoever honors her will have the favor of God as well as her own.)

> *La Virgin gloriosa, estrella de la mar,*
> *Sabe a sus amigos gualardon bueno dar:*
> *Bien sabe a los buenos el bien gualardonar,*
> *A los que la dessierven sabelos mal curar.*

> *Amigos a tal madre aguardarla devemos:*
> *Si a ella sirvieremos nuestra pro buscaremos,*
> *Onrraremos los cuerpos, las almas salvaremos,*
> *Por pocco de servicio grand galardon prendemos.*

(The Glorious Virgin, star of the sea, knows how to give to her devotees a plenteous bounty. Well does she know how to reward them; she knows how to destroy those who render her disservice. My friends, we should cleave to such a mother. If we will serve her, we shall find our own reward, we shall bring honor to our bodies, we shall save our souls. In exchange for a little service we shall obtain a great recompense.)

(Quatrains 73–74)

The Latin states in its usual straightforward way that the Virgin honored Hyldefonsus, and that whoever honors her will have her favor and that of God. No mention is made of the fate of those who do not serve her well. The Spanish says as much and far more. Ildefonso is not even mentioned in the closing lines, perhaps because Berceo felt that his audiences or readers were well informed about him already. Instead, the Spanish speaks of how well the Virgin serves good people and punishes those who render her disservice. The last quatrain, returning to the first person plural, makes it plain that "we, friends," that is, all mankind, should "cleave to such a mother." We are left with a promise, barely mentioned in the Latin: that "we shall find our own reward, we shall bring honor to our bodies, we shall save our souls," provided, of course, that we serve her well. Berceo, then, skillfully weaves into his dénouement a vitality of expression and a depth of belief and emotion well calculated to move his readers and those who heard his miracles read.

II *Berceo and His Audience*

Berceo made, as has been mentioned above, a definite attempt to appeal to his public, using Spanish itself which had been so long used for lengthy narrative poems. In his work, however, perhaps to lend dignity, he substituted for the *mester de juglaría* with assonance and irregularity of syllabification, the *mester de clerecía* with its counted syllables and fully-rhymed quatrains. To be erudite and dignified as to poetic structure, yet popular in listener appeal seems to have been his aim. In quatrain 2 of his *Vida de Santo Domingo de Silos (Life of St. Dominic of Silos),* he wrote: [7]

> I want to write a piece in polished Romance,
> In which the people are accustomed to speak to their neighbors,
> For I am not learned enough to write one in Latin,
> It would indeed be worth, as I believe, a glass of good wine.

> *(Quiero fer una prosa en roman paladino,*
> *En el qual suele el pueblo fablar con su vecino.*
> *Ca non so tan letrado por fer otro latino,*
> *Bien valdra, commo creo, un vaso du buen vino.)*

This passage seems to state conclusively that he regarded the Spanish vernacular—for *roman paladino* (polished romance) meant to him good Spanish as opposed to Latin—as best suited to the establishment of rapport with his public.

His use of this poetic medium, in a sense, bridged the gap between folk poetry, as represented by the epic-like poems written in the *mester de juglaría,* and the poetry of the literate and of the erudite. The *mester de clerecía* could be read by educated people and be respected by them; but, since this poetic form was written in the language understandable among the illiterate, it could be enjoyed, when read or recited, by these people. During Berceo's century, as well as in the fourteenth, this medium was in great vogue for narrative poems of various sorts. The *Libro de Apolonio (Book of Apolonius)* and the *Libro de Alexandre (Book of Alexander)*, both regarded as of definite learned tradition, were written in *cuaderna vía*. Even the *Poema de Fernán González (Poem of Fernán González)*, an epic-like poem whose content had possibly first appeared in the popular *mester de juglaría,* appeared in Berceo's time in the learned poets' medium.[8] And the *Libro de buen amor (Book of Good Love)* of Juan Ruiz, Archpriest of Hita, would go even further in the next century, couching in *cuaderna vía* a vast potpourri of subject matter—learned, popular, satiric, devout, scurrilous, pious, serious, and jocose. *Cuaderna vía,* then, for close to two full centuries encompassed writings of a wide variety.

Berceo in his *Milagros* was following a trend. Interest in epics was on the wane, since the subject matter of epics—wars with the Moors and the emergence of heroes and founders of noble and royal lines—was not as relevant as in earlier times and held less interest for the people. To replace such epics as the *Lay of the Cid,* writers turned to new subjects set down in verse, even as in verse they clung to the age-old themes. Ballads treating the subject matter of epics would be written in the next century, and can be assumed to have been extant in oral tradition even in the thirteenth. Another replacement of epic-type poems were pious writings which attained great popularity, as might be expected, given the popularity in Latin of such writings in most of Europe. The lives and deeds of the saints and the miracles of the Virgin Mary, as has been mentioned earlier, were among the most frequently written. Such subjects lent themselves quite well to lengthy narrative; indeed, to epic-like treatment. They soon became the inspiration for a large body of literature in the vernaculars, and continued to be written also in Latin, even as the vernacular literatures developed. The reasons for such interest were several and some have been touched upon previously. In the case of Berceo's saints' lives, a complexity of reasons may exist. But for the *Milagros de Nuestra Señora,* it is difficult to see any motives other than devotion and piety and the desire to lead men to see the grace, power, and benevolence of the Virgin.

In the *Milagros,* Berceo seems constantly to struggle to please a simple and devout medieval public, with no special class in mind, but rather all classes. The poet keeps his style simple and direct. He employs numerous elements of his native Castilian dialect, using colloquial phrases, diminutives indigenous to the region of La Rioja, a homely, but extremely extensive vocabulary, and numerous proverbial expressions seemingly plucked from the folk speech of his parishioners. He imparts a quality of innocence, of ingenuousness, even of primitivism to the *Milagros* and to all of his works which must surely have been attractive to the people of his own region and age. Even today this primitive, pristine quality is pleasing. To maintain rapport through the avoidance of the monotony so often found in pious writings, Berceo was able to contrast passages of stark and earthy realism with lines that rise above the mundane to heights of near-mysticism; he infused his pages with pathos as well as humor; he wrote his *Milagros,* then, for all people, for the folk of La Rioja and for the folk everywhere, but also for whatever educated person might care to read his works or hear them read.

III *The Remarkable Prologue—an Allegory*

The format of the *Milagros* can be summarized briefly. Some 2744 verses present the twenty-five miracles. These vary in length from 650 verses to forty, although the majority of the miracles range from fifty to eighty.

The miracles are preceded by the most consciously artistic part of the entire book; that is, by a preface or introduction which lays the groundwork for the presentation of the miracles themselves. This introduction is a delightful and lovely allegory in which the excellences of the Virgin are presented to the reader. Berceo paints a charming *locus amoenus,* or "pleasance," as it was called in medieval English writings,[9] a garden or meadow filled with flowers, running streams, replete with trees and birds and their endless song. Such descriptions were famous, and were one of the most beloved and frequently presented topoi of medieval letters. The poet, speaking directly to his audience, offers a picturesque and charming scene indeed.[10] We present the first several quatrains in English and in Spanish to illustrate the poet's skill in his native language:

Friends and vassals of Almighty God,
If you of your own consent will listen to me,
I should like to recount to you a great event;
You will regard it in toto as something truly good.

(Amigos e Vasallos de Dios ominpotent,
Si vos me escuchassedes por vuestro consiment,
Querria vos contar un buen aveniment:
Terrédeslo en cabo por bueno verament.)

I, Master Gonzalo de Berceo by name
Came upon a meadow while I was on pilgrimage,
Green and truly fragrant, well peopled with flowers.
A spot desirable to every man.

(Yo maestro Gonçalvo de Verçeo nomnado,
Iendo en romeria caeçi en un prado
Verde e bien sençido, de flores bien poblado,
Logar cobdiçiaduero pora omne cansado.)

The very aromatic flowers gave forth much perfume;
They refreshed the faces and the spirits of men,
Clear and running streams bathed every stone,
In summer cold, indeed, in winter they were hot.

(Daban olor soveio las flores bien olientes,
Refrescavan en omne las caras e las mientes,
Manavan cada canto fuentes claras corrientes,
En verano bien frias, en yvierno calientes.)

There was a great quantity of fine groves,
Pomegranates and fig trees, pears and apple trees,
And many other fruit trees of diverse coin;
But none were spoiled or bitter.

(Avie hi grand abondo de buenas arboledas,
Milgranos e figueras, peros e mazanedas,
E muchas otras fructas de diversas monedas;
Mas non avie ningunas podridas nin azedas.)

The verdure of the meadow, the fragrance of the flowers,
The shade of the trees with its muted delight
Completely refreshed me and I ceased to perspire:
A man could live on those aromas.

(La verdura del prado, la olor de las flores,
Las sombras de los arbores de temprados sabores
Refrescaron me todo, e perdi los sudores:
Podrie vevir el omne con aquellos olores.)

Never did I find in the world a place so delightful,
Nor shade so mild, nor fragrance so heady.
I removed my garments so as to rest more luxuriously,
And stretched out beneath a lovely tree.

(Nunqua trobé en sieglo logar tan deleitoso,
Nin sombra tan temprada, ni olor tan sabroso.
Descargue mi ropiella por iazer más viçioso,
Poseme a la sombra de un arbor fermoso.)

Lying in the shade I lost all care,
I heard the sweet and modulated bird song.
Men never heard organs more harmonious,
Nor able to produce more harmonious melodies.

(Yaziendo a la sombra perdi todos cuidados,
Odi sonos de aves dulces e modulados:
Nunqua udieron omnes organos más temprados,
Nin que formar pudiessen sones más acordados.)

This meadow, the reader begins to comprehend, is no everyday patch of verdure, and Berceo tells us that this is true.

The meadow of which I speak had another virtue:
It would not lose its beauty through heat or cold,
It was always green in its entirety,
It would not lose its verdure through any storm.

(El prado que vos digo avie otra bondat:
Por calor nin por frio non perdie su beltat,
Siempre estava verde en su entegredat,
Non perdie la verdura por nulla tempestat.)

As soon as I lay down upon the ground
I was immediately relieved of all weariness:
I forgot all care, all past wretchedness:
Whoever might rest here would be happy.

(Man a mano que fuy en tierra acostado,
De todo el lazerio fui luego folgado :
Oblidé toda cuita, el lazerio passado :
¡Qui alli se morasse serie bien venturado!)

Whatever men and birds came here
Could carry off as many of the flowers as they pleased.
Nor would they cause any decrease in the meadow,
For each one they plucked, three or four sprang up.

(Los omnes e las aves quantas acaecien,
Levavan de las flores quantas levar querien ;
Mas mengua en el prado niguna non façien :
Por una que levavan, tres e quatro nazien.)

This meadowland seemed like paradise
In which God has placed so much grace and so much benediction.
He who created such a thing was a wise master :
A man who might dwell here would never lose perception.

(Semeia esti prado egual de paraiso,
En qui Dios tan grand graçia, tan grand bendición
El que crió tal cosa, maestro fue anviso :
Omne que hi morasse, nunqua perdrie el viso.)

The fruit of the trees was sweet and tasty.
If Sir Adam had eaten such fruit
He would not have been deceived so badly,
Nor would Eve and her husband have been so damaged.

(El fructo de los arbores era dulz e sabrido,
Si don Adam oviesse de tal fructo comido,
De tan mala manera non serie decibido,
Nin tomarien tal danno Eva ni so marido.)

After dwelling in detail upon birds and fruit, the poet admits
that the pleasance he has described is divine.

Good folk and friends, what we have said
Is obscure in meaning and we wish to explain it.
Let us remove the hull and penetrate to the fruit.
Let us take what is inside, let us leave the outer covering.

(Sennores e amigos, lo que dicho avemos,
Palabra es oscura, esponerla queremos:
Tolgamos la corteza, al meollo entremos,
Prendamos lo de dentro, lo de fuera dessemos.)

All of us who are alive and go about on two feet,
Whether in prison we lie, or in a bed,
All of us are pilgrims who travel a highway:
St. Peter says this, through him we prove it.

(Todos quantos vevimos que en piedes andamos,
Si quiere en preson, o en lecho iagamos.
Todos somos romeos que camino andamos:
San Peidro lo diz esto, por él vos lo provamos.)

All of us who live here, live in someone else's power:
We await the everlasting abode in heaven;
We end our pilgrimage then
When we send our souls to paradise.

(Quanto aqui vivimos, en ageno moramos;
La ficança durable suso la esperamos,
La nuestra romeria estonz la acabamos
Quando a paraiso las almas enviamos.)

On this pilgrimage we have a good meadowland
In which every weary pilgrim finds a refuge:
the Glorious Virgin, Mother of the good Son,
For whom no other equal has been found.

(En esta romeria avemos un buen prado,
En qui trova repaire tot romeo cansado,
La Virgin Gloriosa, madre del buen criado,
Del qual otro ninguno egual non fué trobado.)

This meadow was always green in purity,
For never did her virginity have any taint,
Post partum et in partu was she a true virgin,
Stainless, incorrupt in her integrity.

(Esti prado fué siempre verde en onestat,
Ca nunca ovo macula la su virginidat,
Post partum et in partu fue Virgin de verdat,
Illesa, incorrupta en su entegredat.)

The four clear streams which watered the meadow
Signified the four Gospels,
For four Evangelists who wrote them,
When they penned them, they spoke with her.

(Las quatro fuentes claras que del prado manavan,
Los quatro evangelios esso significavan,
Ca los evangelistas quantro que los dictavan,
Quando los escrivien, con ella se fablaban.)

He continues, giving even more detailed observations and explanations as to what he finds in the pleasance:

The shadows of the trees, good, sweet and healthful,
In which all pilgrims take shelter,
These are the prayers which St. Mary says,
Since she prays for sinners night and day.

La sombra de los arbores, buena, dulze sania,
En qui ave repaire toda la romeria,
Si son las oraciones que faz Santa Maria,
Que por los peccadores ruega noch e dia.)

All in the world, the just and the sinners,
Clerics and laymen, kings and emperors;
There all of us run, vassals and lords,
We all go under her sway to gather flowers.

(Quantos que son en mundo iustos e peccadores,
Coronados e legos, reys e enperadores
Alli corremos todos vassallos e sennores,
Todos a la su sombra imos coger las flores.)

The trees which make the sweet and pleasant shade
Are the holy miracles which the Glorious One performs,
For these are much sweeter than the delicious sugar
Which they give to the sick in grievous travail.

(Los arbores que facen sombra dulz e donosa,
Son los santos miraclos que faz la Gloriosa,
Ca son mucho más dulzes que azucar sabrosa,
La que dan al enfermo en la cuita raviosa.)

The birds which carol among the fruit trees
Which have such sweet voices, sing devout songs,
These are Augustine, Gregory and the other saints
Who set down in writing her noble deeds.

(Las aves que organan entre essos fructales,
Que an las dulzes vozes, dicen cantos leales,
Estos son Agustint, Gregorio, otros tales,
Quantos que escrivieron los sos fechos reales.)

These maintain love and friendship with her,
They put all their energy into praising her actions,
They all speak about her, each one his part;
But they all have in all this a single creed.

(Estos avien con ella amor e atenencia,
En laudar los sos fechos metien toda femencia,
Todos fablaban della, cascuno su sentencia;
Pero tenien por todo todos una creencia.)

Than the nightingale which carols with delicate art
And even the calander lark which sings so melodiously,
Much better sang the Prophet Isaiah
And the other Prophets, a noble company.

(El rosennor que canta por fina maestria,
Siquiere la calandria que faz grand melodia,
Mucho cantó meior el varon Ysaya,
E los otros prophetas, onrrada conpania.)

The Apostles sang quite natural melodies,
Confessors and martyrs sang similar ones,
The virgins came behind the great all-powerful Mother,
They chant before her a most festive song.

(Cantaron los apostolos muedo mui natural,
Confessores e martires facien bien otro tal,
Las virgines siguieron la grand Madre caudal,
Cantan delante della canto vien festival.)

Through all the churches, and this each day,
All the clergy sings lauds before her:

All pay court to the Virgin Mary:
These are nightingales of extreme charm.

(Por todas las eglesias, esto es cada dia,
Cantan laudes antella toda la clerecia :
Todos li façen cort a la Virgo Maria :
Estos son rossennoles de grand plaçenteria.)

Let us return to the flowers which cover the meadow,
For they make it lovely, beautiful and harmonious:
The flowers are the names which Scripture gives
To the Virgin Mary, Mother of the good Son.

(Tornemos ennas flores que conponen el prado,
Que lo façen fermoso, apuesto e temprado :
Las flores son los nomnes que li da el dictado
A la Virgo Maria, madre del buen criado.)

Berceo continues beyond this explanation with other names of
the Virgin—Stella Maris, Temple of Jesus Christ, Morning Star,
David's Slingshot, etc.
He reaches a denouement in two telling quatrains:

I should like to climb up for a while into these trees,
And to write about some of her miracles,
May the Glorious One guide me to do so,
For I would not dare to enter upon it.

(Quiero en estos arbores un ratiello sobir,
E de los sos miraclos algunos escrivir,
La Gloriosa me guie que lo pueda complir,
Ca yo non me trevria en ello a venir.)

I shall consider it a miracle which the Glorious one performs,
If she should wish to guide me in this thing:
Mother, full of grace, puissant Queen,
Thou guidest me in it, for thou art merciful.

(Terrélo por miraculo que lo faz la Gloriosa
Si guiarme quisiere a mi en esta cosa:
Madre plena de gracia, Reyna poderosa,
Tu me guia en ello, ca eres piadosa.)

The last quatrain in the introduction sets the stage for the first miracle:

> In Spain I desire then to commence:
> In Toledo the Great, a famous place,
> For I do not know where else to begin to speak,
> Since they are more numerous than the sands of the sea.

> (*En Espanna cobdicio de luego empezar:*
> *En Toledo la magna, un famado logar,*
> *Ca non sé de qual cabo empieze a contar,*
> *Ca más son que arenas en riba de la mar.*)

IV *The Format and Presentation of the Miracles*

The very first miracle, to which we give the title "La Casulla de San Ildefonso" ("St. Ildefonso's Chasuble") indeed begins in Toledo, as we have seen earlier, when this miracle was compared with its Latin source:

> In Toledo the Good, that royal town,
> Which lies above the Tajo, that copious stream,
> There was an archbishop, a faultless cleric,
> Who was the Glorious One's loyal friend.
> They called him Ildefonso, the writings say so.

> (*En Toledo la buena, essa villa real*
> *Que iaze sobre Taio, essa agua cabdal,*
> *Ovo un arzobispo, coronado leal,*
> *Que fue de la Gloriosa amigo natural.*
> *Dizienli Yldefonso, dizlo la escriptura.*)

A more or less set pattern serves in the presentation of each miracle. As can be seen from the opening stanzas of the first miracle, the poet lays the scene, giving the name of the city and the name of the protagonist. He then describes the protagonist and acquaints us with his qualities.

> They call him Ildefonso, the writings say it,
> a shepherd who provided good pasturage for his flock,
> A man of saintly life who practiced great tenderness

(Dizienli Yldefonso, dizlo la escriptura,
Pastor que a su grei dava buena pastura:
Omne de sancta vida que trásco grand cordura.)

Those of evil intent receive graphic treatment also, as can be
seen, for example, in Miracle 20, "El Clerigo Embriagado" ("The
Drunken Cleric"):

He entered a wineshop one day perchance,
He drank much wine, this without moderation,
The fool became drunk, he went out of his wits,
He lay until vespers on the hard ground.

(Entró enna bodega un dia por ventura,
Bebió mucho del bino, esto fo sin mesura,
Embebdóse el locco, issió de su cordura,
Iogó hasta las viesperas sobre la tierra dura.)
(Quatrain 463)

If some truly evil antagonist is a character, he, too, is presented
early by the poet, as can be seen in Miracle 8, "El Romero de
Santiago" ("The Pilgrim of St. James"), in which the devil himself
appears to a sinner:

The devil was always the ancient enemy:
He is a wise master of every wickedness;
He seems at times an angel of God;
And he is a sly devil, a wicked seducer,
.
He transformed himself, the false one, into a true angel,
And appeared before him in the midst of the path.
"Welcome be your coming," he said to the pilgrim,
"You seem to me to be as innocent as a lamb."

(El diablo antigo sienpre fo traidor,
Es de toda nemiga maestro sabidor,
Semeia a las vezes angel del Criador,
E es diablo fino de mal sosacador,

Transformóse el falso en angel verdadero,
Parose li delante en medio un sendero:
"Bien seas tu venido—dissoli al romero—
Semeiasme cossiella simple como cordero.")
(Quatrains 187–188)

After such introductory scenes and characterizations, the miracle runs its course, ending almost invariably with one or more quatrains which relate the reward for piety and devotion or the punishment for sin and a reminder that the Virgin is a constant protectress. A graphic example of this is the closing of the miracle known as "La Abadesa Encinta" ("The Pregnant Abbess"), Number 21:

> When the time came in which she was to die,
> She (the Virgin) did not let her soul languish for long;
> She took her up to Glory, a secure abode,
> Where neither robber nor tax collector can ever enter.

> *(Quando vino el término que obo de finar,*
> *No lo dessó su Ama luengamiente lazrar:*
> *Levólo a la gloria, a seguro logar,*
> *Do ladron nin merino nunqua puede entrar.)*
> (Quatrain 581)

With an understanding of the almost formulistic manner of presenting a miracle, it will be worthwhile to read in English one complete miracle. Number 9 is representative of the collection. The title is "El Clérigo Ignorante" ("The Ignorant Monk"):

The Ignorant Monk

There was a simple monk and scant of learning, who daily said Mass to Holy Mary. He knew how to say none other, and this he repeated each day, saying it from memory rather than from rote.

This Mass-singer was reported to the bishop, accused of idiocy, and proved to be a bad monk: the poor stupid wretch knew only the *Salva Sancta Parens,* and this alone he said.

The bishop was deeply moved to wrath, and he said:

"I never heard such a thing about a priest! Tell that whore's son to come before me, and let him not plan any trick."

The erring priest appeared before the bishop and from fear he had gone pale. He was unable, out of embarrassment, to meet the eyes of his superior. Never had the wretch been in such a sweat.

"Priest," said the bishop, "tell me the truth as to whether your ignorance is what they say it is."

"Sir," replied the priest, "if I should say otherwise it would be a falsehood."

"Since you have no knowledge about singing Mass," said the bishop, "and no intelligence nor ability, I forbid you to sing it. You are under this sentence! Earn your living, as you deserve to do, in some other calling."

The priest departed sad and confused. He was terribly ashamed and his misfortune was great. Tearful and plaintive he turned to the Glorious One for advice, for he was frightened.

The Wondrous Mother who never failed one who cast himself at her feet with sincerity, listened straightway to the prayers of her priest. She did not allot any appointed time: she came to his aid immediately. In a vision the Glorious Virgin Mother without stain appeared to the bishop. She preached to him strong words, a quite fiery sermon. She made her feelings very plain to him.

"Sir hasty bishop," she said angrily, "why hast thou been so hard and so cruel to me? Never did I do thee a jot of harm. And thou hast removed my chaplain! Thou thoughtest the one who used to sing Mass to me was committing the sin of heresy. Thou consideredest him a dumb beast and a sinner and thou tookest from him the duty of chaplain. I shall have a great quarrel with thee if thou dost not command him to sing my Masses. And thou shalt die thirty days hence. In this matter shalt thou see the power of Holy Mary!"

Terrified by these threats the bishop immediately summoned the discharged priest. He besought him to forgive the error he had made, for he had been sadly deceived in his sentence. He told him to sing the Mass as he had been accustomed to do, to be the servant of the Glorious One at her altar, and he said that if he ever lacked any vestment or footgear, he would order his own given him.

The good man returned to his chaplainship and served the Glorious Mother, Holy Mary, ending his days in his duty, as I hope to end mine. His soul went to its glory and to the fraternity of the blessed.

We would be unable to set down or recite, even though we lived a long life, one-tenth of the miracles which God wrought for that Glorious Lady.[11]

As has been stated earlier, there are twenty-five miracles. Almost all are of international medieval currency and most were well known and much cited in medieval literatures. Even though it will not be feasible to give a lengthy outline of each miracle, it will be well, at least, to list their titles, with short sketches of their content.

V *List of the Miracles*

1. "St. Ildefonso's Chasuble" ("La Casulla de San Yldefonso"). Herein a chasuble, given by the Virgin to St. Ildefonso, strangles a priest who took possession of it after the saint's death.
2. "The Unchaste Sacristan" ("El Sacristán Impúdico"). A sac-

ristan drowns as he leaves his mistress, and his soul is seized by devils. The Virgin restores it because he had been a devotee.

3. "The Cleric and the Flower" ("El Clérigo y la Flor"). An ignorant priest is buried in the potters' field, and when exhumed at the Virgin's command, is found incorrupt with a marvelous blossom growing from his mouth.

4. "The Virgin's Reward" ("El Premio de la Virgen"). A devotee, who is a cleric, writes songs in Mary's honor. When he dies, she conducts his soul to paradise.

5. "The Poor Almsgiver" ("El Pobre Caritativo"). A poor man who shares his all with other poor folk is personally taken to heaven by the Virgin.

6. "The Devout Robber" ("El Ladrón Devoto"). When the authorities hanged a robber who had always praised the Virgin, she supported his weight on her hands and kept him alive on the gallows. Later her hands protect his neck from the executioner.

7. "The Monk and St. Peter" ("El Monje y San Pedro"). A monk begets a child and later dies. St. Peter tries to get the monk into heaven. Jesus will not permit his entry until the Virgin asks it of Him.

8. "St. James's Pilgrim" ("El Romero de Santiago"). A sinful pilgrim, deceived by the devil into emasculating himself, dies. He is resuscitated by the Virgin, minus the organs that sinned.

9. "The Ignorant Monk" ("El Clérigo Ignorante"). A monk too ignorant to learn any Mass save that of the Virgin, is cast out by his bishop, but reinstated at the Virgin's command.

10. "The Two Brothers" ("Los Dos Hermanos"). One brother, a good man, beseeches his saint to take his sinful brother's soul to heaven. The saint appeals to the Virgin and she to God with success.

11. "The Avaricious Farmer" ("El Labrador Avaro"). The soul of a money-mad farmer is carried off by devils but is saved by the Virgin, since he had revered her.

12. "The Prior and the Sacristan" ("El Prior y el Sacristán"). A faithful sacristan tells how his prior was saved from hell by the Virgin who went to retrieve his soul.

13. "The New Bishop" ("El Obispo Nuevo"). The Virgin nominates Jerónimo, a poor hermit, to be bishop, and on her advice he is elected.

14. "The Respected Image" ("La Imagen Respetada"). An entire monastery burns, but the image of the Virgin and the Child are unharmed.
15. "The Wedding and the Virgin" ("La Boda y la Virgen"). A young canon left the church to marry, but the Virgin prevented the consummation of the wedding and he returned to holy orders.
16. "The Jewish Lad" ("El Niño Judío"). A Jewish student, cast into a furnace by his own father for taking Communion, is protected from the flames by the Virgin.
17. "The Profaned Church" ("La Iglesia Profanada"). Three knights who slay a fourth in the sanctuary of a church are punished, but receive forgiveness from the Virgin.
18. "The Jews of Toledo" ("Los Judíos de Toledo"). Jews are arrested and punished when the Virgin's voice advises authorities that in the ghetto a crucifix is being profaned.
19. "A Miraculous Birth" ("Un Parto Maravilloso"). A pregnant woman unable to get to shore from the sea is saved by the Virgin who serves as midwife and delivers the woman's child.
20. "The Drunken Cleric" ("El Clérigo Embriagado"). The Virgin drives off the devil who appears in several animal forms to threaten a drunken monk.
21. "The Pregnant Abbess" ("La Abadesa Encinta"). The Virgin delivers the abbess's child, concealing the birth miraculously from the bishop.
22. "The Shipwrecked Sailor Saved" ("El Náufrago Salvado"). The Virgin casts a cloth to a shipwrecked sailor, her devotee, and it carries him to shore.
23. "The Debt Paid" ("La Deuda Pagada"). A Jew who receives miraculously from the sea the money owed him by a Christian, refuses to admit payment. When an image of the Child Jesus reveals the matter, the Jew is convicted.
24. "The Miracle of Theophilus" ("El Milagro de Teófilo"). The Virgin saves the soul of Theophilus who had bartered it to the devil for power and wealth.
25. "The Pillaged Church" ("La Iglesia Robada"). Robbers who desecrate the church they are robbing and also the Virgin's image, are miraculously held until the authorities come.

The *Milagros de Nuestra Señora,* Berceo's greatest contribution to Marian literature in Spain's thirteenth century, was not equalled in Castilian in that century or in subsequent ages. More erudite, more copious, and more lyrical are King Alfonso X's *Cantigas de Santa María,* but these are written in Galician-Portuguese rather than in Spanish. Together they make the thirteenth century rich in the recounting of the miracles of the Blessed Virgin.

CHAPTER 4

La Vida de San Millán de la Cogolla

I *Berceo's Reasons for Writing this* Vida

L A Vida de San Millán de la Cogolla (Life of St. Aemilianus of
La Cogolla) is possibly the first attempt Berceo made to write
in the area of saints' lives. He must have felt particularly at home,
even so, for as he penned the 1900-odd verses or 499 quatrains, he
could gaze from the window of his cell or from the casement of
the monastery library at the very scenes which had been familiar
to St. Aemilianus, [1] who died in 574, and ranked among the notable
ecclesiastics of the late Visigothic era in Spain. He flourished just
before the cultural awakening set in motion by St. Isidore of Seville
(570?–636) and was considered important enough to merit a biography written by no less a personage than St. Isidore's disciple,
St. Braulius, Bishop of Saragossa. It was understandable, then,
that Berceo felt a deep personal pride in the saint who had founded
the very monastery which meant so much to him. By the mid-
thirteenth century when Berceo was writing, and even from long
before, the life and miracles of Aemilianus had had time to assume
all the attributes of tradition, legend, and local folklore. After all,
some 600-odd years had passed, and the memory of the saint had
become a familiar part of the fabric of life in La Rioja. Berceo, no
doubt, knew the legends and the folk beliefs, and most certainly
he had perused the documents which set down the life and miracles
of Aemilianus. His first saint's life was based upon a manuscript of
the *Vita Beati Aemiliani (Life of Blessed Aemilianus)* which Braulius
had composed in Latin prose so long before, and this document
verified in Berceo's mind the belief that Aemilianus himself had
founded the monastery which later bore his name. Quite probably
the saint was, indeed, the actual founder of the monastery, although
this cannot be proven, since no monastic document earlier than
924 is extant, and this document states only that King Garci
Sánchez of Nájera granted the parish church of Santa María de
Cañas to the monastery. [2] No mention is made of any previously
established monastic house in the village of Berceo.

A long tradition about San Millán, then, had developed by
Berceo's time, and the poet quite obviously had steeped himself
in it. He knew the region's history and the great events his monastery had seen, from the time it stood on its original site in the
mountains and then from a later period when it was reestablished
on the plain near Berceo. Heroes, like Fernán González, had do-
nated to it, as had certain of the kings of Navarre. Moorish armies
led by Almanzor, Caliph of Cordova, had in the year 1002 sacked
and burned the monastery. Monarchs of Navarre, however, had,
during the eleventh century, restored and embellished it.[3] After
all, San Millán had become a patron of Navarrese and Castilian
peoples. Indeed, in Berceo's own time someone had written an
epic poem in *cuaderna vía,* the *Poema de Fernán González,* in which
San Millán appeared in battle against the Moslems.

In 1030 the remains of the saint had been exhumed from the
tomb in the cave where he had sequestered himself while he lived,
and had been given honored entombment under the altar in the
monastery church. Berceo knew, also, as would have any inhabitant
of so sacred a place, that in 1053, a king of Navarre had begun a
new church and a new monastic house on the plain near the village
of Berceo and had carried it to conclusion by 1067. For a while,
Berceo knew, both the old monastery and the new had functioned,
almost within sight of one another, the old one called "San Millán
de Suso" (Upper St. Millán) and the new "San Millán de Yuso"
(Lower St. Millán).

Berceo surely assessed the situation of his beloved monastery,
and must have realized, as did all the clergy concerned, that the
age-old prosperity of San Millán was waning. Pilgrims still appeared, but their numbers grew smaller. Many preferred the more
recent, and probably more popular centers of pilgrimage wherein
accommodations may have been better. The situation of San
Millán was critical and clearly something had to be done. Brian
Dutton has established with considerable certainty that something
was done, and that quite probably Berceo, among others, worked
hard to improve the monastery's situation and to reinstate it as an
effective shrine. Dutton points to numerous false documents written
to enrich the monastery.[4] Some of these documents sought to
convince patrons and others who had promised donations, or who
might be led to subscribe, that St. Millán himself was ever ready to
reward the generous or punish the stingy. Other documents at-

tempted, apparently with great success, to prevent various bishops from claiming tithes and levies from the monastery's coffers. Pope Innocent IV himself in 1245 was asked to arbitrate and, deceived by false documents, his appointed judges were led to rule in favor of the monastery and against those who made claims against it.

The most startling falsification, and the one which brought most honor and wealth to San Millán, was the copy of the vows of donation to the saint, vows which sought to force all the towns of Castile and in parts of Aragon and Navarre to pay an annual quota to the monastery. The documents alleged that Fernán González, the local region's great epic hero, had founded the monastery in 934. It was like proving today that George Washington or Abraham Lincoln had founded a church in America. The results were most gratifying to the monks, since great prosperity came to San Millán thereafter.

Dutton believes that Berceo, who lived through the period of falsification of documents, may actually have been the notary of Abbot Juan Sánchez of San Millán, and that quite possibly Berceo engaged actively in such falsifications. A kinder view might be that the simple Berceo, if he were as simple as such scholars as Menéndez y Pelayo and Valbuena Prat believe him to have been,[5] merely copied what the abbot handed him, or wrote down what the abbot told him to write, accepting it for truth. This is difficult to accept, however, when one considers Berceo's familiarity with monastic holdings at St. Millán and the knowledge he must have had about the case. But even if the poet falsified willingly, or allowed himself to be used by the falsifiers, he might well have considered that the end justified the means. Those who are interested in such matters may read a complete and convincing account of them in the Primera Parte of Dr. Dutton's book cited earlier. The entire matter is pertinent, of course, to those who read Berceo, because it poses a new and practical reason for the writing of one of Berceo's most famous saints' lives, *La Vida de San Millán de la Cogolla*. This contradicts, of course, the hitherto accepted reasons attributed to Berceo's commendable and pious desire to honor the patron saint of his own monastery and to glorify the Holy Trinity and the Blessed Virgin, who stood behind the saintly Aemilianus. Dutton points to page and line in *La Vida de San Millán* to support his supposition:

He who wishes to learn about the life at San Millán,
And to be very certain of his history,
Let him set his mind upon what I wish to state:
He will see where the folk send their money.

According to my belief, let it grieve the Devil!
At last, when the tract has been read,
He will learn such things as will please him,
He will not be sorry to give three mites.

(Qui la vida quisiere de Sant Millán saber,
E de la su ystoria bien certano seer,
Meta mientes en esto que yo quiero leer,
Verá a do envian los pueblos so aver.

Secundo mi creencia que pese al pecado,
En cabo quando fuere leydo el dictado,
Aprendrá tales cosas de que será pagado,
De dar las tres meajas non li será pasado.)
                            (Quatrains 1–2)

The donations to San Millán certainly are alluded to in the fourth line of the first quatrain; and surely the last line in the second quatrain refers to small donations; donations to the monastery and not to some troubadour, which latter supposition was strongly supported by Menéndez Pidal.[6]

It can be seen, then, that Berceo may have composed his *Vida de San Millán* for more than one reason: out of piety and a desire to honor the local saint and the monastery he was believed to have founded, thereby attracting pilgrims to his shrine; or, because Berceo believed that such writing could lead people to pay the donations they had agreed to pay. Whatever his reason, he produced an interesting document based upon a five-hundred-year-old Latin writing.

II *Berceo's Art in the* Vida

Berceo's Spanish rendition of the *Vita Beati Aemiliani* differed as greatly from the Latin prose account set down by St. Braulius, as had his *Milagros de Santa Maria* from its Latin original. The same embellishment of the simple Latin, the same use of local color, proverbial phrases, the quaint and rustic vocabulary of La Rioja, and Berceo's own particular handling of Castilian syntax are to be found. And, of course, the same poetic demands of the *mester de clerecía* regulated the poem's presentation.

Berceo as a priest knew his parishioners well, and no doubt realized how valuable close and intimate affinity with his people could be. Therefore, in his works, particularly in the *Vida de San Millán de la Cogolla,* he wrote in a manner designed to identify himself as a member of a simple religious community:

> Gonzalo was the name of the one who wrote this tract.
> He was from childhood brought up in Upper San Millán.
> He was a native of Berceo, where San Millán was born.
> May God guard his soul from the devil's power.
>
> *(Gonzalo fue so nombre qui fizo est tractado.*
> *En Sant Millan de Suso fue de niño criado.*
> *Natural de Berceo, ond Sant Millan fue nado.*
> *Dios guarde la su alma del poder del peccado.)*
> (Quatrain 489)

Berceo, then, was educated at San Millán, quite probably in a monastic school conducted there, or perhaps he studied under the private tutelage of some of the brethren. As a local product, he was especially well fitted to render into the native patois the life of the most famous of local saints. He writes as though he were a simple man making an effort to establish and maintain rapport with an unsophisticated public. It has been said by scholars that he deliberately interprets himself as a poorly educated person, and that this is a simulated ignorance designed to attract folk who would have been reticent and embarrassed before a learned poet. There is reason for such a belief about Berceo, for he was certainly not the ignorant priest he professed to be. He read Latin very well indeed, it would appear, and he had the vocabulary and poetic skill of a trained writer. And yet, even if his simplicity was simulated, and even though he was far from an unscholarly man, he seems to have been nonetheless deeply pious and devoted in his faith in the Virgin and in the powers of his saints.

III *The Structure of the* Vida de San Millán

Berceo structured all of his saints' lives in a tripartite pattern[7] and according to a conscious plan, although variations occur from *vida* to *vida*. In so doing he was not demonstrating originality, for age-old custom in the compositions of hagiographical writing dictated such structuring. The typical *vita sancti* (saint's life) in those times was divided into three parts: the saint's background, parentage etc., together with a miraculous announcement of his future greatness; his childhood and youth, his deeds as a man, his virtues and the miracles he wrought while alive; the veneration given him and the miracles after his death.[8]

Berceo adhered fairly closely to this plan in his own *vidas*. In the *Vida de San Millán de la Cogolla* he wrote toward the close of the first part:

> Gentlemen, thanks to God, we have recounted to you
> As much as we know about the holy recluse,
> And about his actions according as we read it:
> Therefore, if you please, it is time for us to rest.

> *(Sennores, Deo graçias, contadovos avemos*
> *Del sancto solaterio quanto saber podemos,*
> *E de las sues andadas secund lo que leemos:*
> *Desaqui, si quisieredes, ora es de que folguemos.)*
> (Quatrain 108)

After this "rest" or pause, the poet begins the second part of the *vida:*

> If, gentlemen, you still should wish to listen,
> The second book is all to be recited:
> I would like to relate a few miracles to you,
> Which God deigned to show to the world through him.

> *(Aun si mi quisieredes, sennores, escuchar,*
> *El secundo libriello todo es de rezar:*
> *Unos pocos miraclos vos querría contar,*
> *Que dennó Dios al mundo por elli demonstrar.)*
> (Quatrain 109)

As would be expected, from what has been said above, a third section or part concludes the *vida*. Berceo ends his second part and uses what today would be called in writers' terminology a "narrative hook," readying the reader for the dénouement and arousing his interest:

Gentlemen, I still wish to continue with this tale,
With him still guiding me, I wish to speak to you about him;
The material is lengthy, about a worthy man;
It would be a great failing to cut it short.

(Sennores, aun quiero desta razon tractar,
Aun él me guiando, dél vos quiero fablar,
La materia es larga de omne de prestar,
Serie grant menoscabo por vos la destaiar.)
            (Quatrain 320)

With this indication that there is more to follow, Berceo opens the third part of the *vida* with an introductory passage:

We have the third part to recount
About precious miracles delightful to hear;
If your goodness were such as that you would wish to continue with me,
I do not wish too quickly to bid you farewell.

(El tercer libriello avemos de deçir
De preçiosos miraclos sabroso de oyr:
Si fuere vuestra gracia quem querades soffrir,
Non quiero tan ayna de vos me despedir.)
            (Quatrain 321)

Berceo was well aware of the symbolic justification for the tri-partite division of his *vida,* knowing that his audience would quickly make the necessary association with the Holy Trinity. He did not, however, actually make the parallels apparent in the *Vida de San Millán,* perhaps because he knew that the comparison was implicit, or perhaps because he simply overlooked the opportunity to state the parallels.

In his second *vida,* however, the *Vida de Santo Domingo de Silos,* Berceo is more explicit, stating plainly that his tripartite division is symbolic of the Trinity:

Gentlemen and friends, may God be praised for it,
We have finished the second book;
We wish to begin another at our pleasure
So that there may be three books, and one complete writing.

Just as there are three persons, and one Divinity.
Which signify the Holy Trinity,
Let there be three books, one truth.
Let the unified material signify the one God.

(Sennores, e amigos, Dios sea end la dado,
El segundo libriello avemos acabado;
Queremos empezar otro a nuestro grado:
Que sean tres los libros, e uno el dictado.

Commo son tres personas, e una Divinidat,
Que sean tres los libros, una certanedat,
Los libros que signifiquen la Sancta Trinidad,
La materia ungada la simple deidat.)
(Quatrains 533–534)

IV *The Presentation of the* Vida

In the first division of the *Vida de San Millán de la Cogolla* we read an interesting account of the saint's life. The poet having invoked, at the outset of his story, God the Father, God the Son, and God, as is the case in all of his *vidas,* the Holy Ghost, begins San Millán's life:

Whoever should like to know of the life of San Millán,
And to be perfectly certain of his story,
Let him pay heed to this which I wish to read.
He will see where the people send their money.

(Qui la vida quisiere de Sant Millan saber,
E de la su ystoria bien certano seer,
Meta mientes en esto que yo quiero leer,
Verá a do envian los pueblos so aver.)
(Quatrain 1)

After this we read that Millán was born and baptized and that as soon as he was old enough, he was sent out as a shepherd to guard his father's sheep. He proved to be a devoted shepherd, protected his sheep well, and with his zither kept himself awake so

that neither wolf nor robber ever was able to steal a sheep. The
account is told with a delightful and biblical directness, as the
following quatrain illustrates:

> He guarded his flock well as one very experienced,
> His crook in his hand in the manner of a shepherd;
> Well did he repel both wolf and evil thief;
> The sheep had great affection for him.
>
> *(Guardaba bien su grey commo muy sabidor,*
> *So cayado en mano a ley de pastor.*
> *Bien referia al lobo e al mal robador:*
> *Las obeias con elli avian muy gran sabor.)*
>   (Quatrain 6)

> The shepherd of whom I speak to you had another custom,
> He always carried with him a zither to use
> To banish sleep, so that the wicked enemy
> Would not be able to steal from him either lamb or kid.
>
> *(Abia otra costumme el pastor que vos digo,*
> *Por uso una çitara traye siempre consigo,*
> *Por referir el suenno, que el mal enemigo*
> *Furtar non li pudiesse cordero nin cabrito.)*
>   (Quatrain 7)

But God had a more important role planned for Millán and He
caused him to fall into a deep sleep from which he awakened instructed to leave his sheep and goats so as to become a holy hermit.
He made his way, still guided by God, to ask St. Felix to instruct
him in the doctrine.

Apparently the shepherd's ignorance was great, and he admitted
this in touching and simple words:

> I know nothing about letters, please understand this,
> I understand naught of the root of sacred belief:
> Father, I beg mercy of you, lying at your feet,
> So that you set your hand to this wretchedness of mine.
>
> *(Non sé nada de letras, vásmelo entendiendo;*
> *De la sancta creençia la raiz non entiendo:*
> *Padre, mercet te clamo, a tos piedes jaçiendo,*
> *Que en esti laçerio vayas mano metiendo.)*
>   (Quatrain 18)

Touching and simple, too, is Millán's personal account of his
humble origins:

> Should you like to know more about the place of my origin,
> I was born in Berceo, which is close to Madrid;
> My good nurse named me Millán;
> Until now I have spent my life with sheep.
>
> *(Demas si saber quieres do vengo la raiz,*
> *En Berçeo fui nado, çerca es de Madriz;*
> *Millán me puso nomme la buena nodriz,*
> *Fasta aqui mie vida con obeias la fiz.)*
>   (Quatrain 19)

In a short time, to St. Felix' delight and amazement, Millán
learned to perfection the Scripture and the prayers and hymns of
the Church; then, to the old saint's sorrow, Millán asked permission to return to the mountains to become a hermit. Probably the
two men never saw one another again, for travel was a difficult and
dangerous activity in the sixth century. At least Berceo questioned
further meetings after the disciple made his return to the mountains:

> Never more do we read nor can we discern
> That these two met again in this life anywhere.
>
> *(Nunqua mas non leemos nin podemos trovar,*
> *Que se iuntassen ambos vivos en un lugar.)*
>   (Quatrain 26)

Millán occupied a cave near Berceo from which he banished
fierce beasts and serpents and then spent a life of prayer and mor-
tification of the flesh. He forgot his relatives and friends and lived
in utter solitude. His whole being was wrapped up in contemplation
and prayers.

> The man endowed with complete goodness,
> Ancient in wisdom, a youth in age,
> Lived in this life with such great sanctity,
> That I cannot tell the half of his virtue.
>
> *(El varon acabado de complida verdat,*
> *Ançiano de seso, mançebo de edat,*

Vivie en esta vida de tan gran sanctidat,
Del so bien non podrie contar la meatat.)
(Quatrain 39)

But his fame spread and people came to visit him in such numbers that he became confused and resolved to steal away by night to find a secluded retreat. He found a lonely hideaway in La Cogolla and lived as a recluse there for forty years:

For forty years he dwelt alone in the mountains,
Never did he have comfort or companionship from man,
Nor food nor clothing, which is a great accomplishment,
No more venerable confessor was born in Spain.

(Quarenta annos visco solo por la montaña,
Nunqua de omne ovo solaz nin companna,
Nin vito nin vestido, que es maior fazanna,
Confessor tan preçioso non nascio en Espanna.)
(Quatrain 63)

However, after the forty years he was summoned by the Bishop of Tarazona, and though unwilling to leave his solitude, Millán descended to the city, where the bishop persuaded him to take religious orders and thereby benefit his fellowman. His only request was that he be allowed to live as a monk in his native region.

He entered the local monastic house of St. Eulalia and lived to improve the lot of the poor, to turn the wicked back into the paths of righteousness, and otherwise to please the Lord; but, quite naturally, he aroused first the envy, and then the rancor, of the brethren. Some of these accused him of crimes he would have considered unspeakable. At last he fled the monastery, betook himself to the wilds of the mountains, built a small chapel, and continued in holiness.

The second division of the *vida* begins with the statement that some miracles will be related, but that only a few from the many can be offered.

We read that Beelzebub, who had been conquered by Millán, assumed human form and confronted him, challenging him to battle. The loser would retreat and relinquish the region to the victor:

As soon as he had said this the irate beast
Tried to lay his angry hands upon the holy man
And to come to grips with him, to hold him hip to hip;
But none of it availed him the value of a wormy walnut.

*(Luego qe esto disso la bestia enconada,
quiso en el (santo) omne meter mano irada,
abraçarce con elli, oararlo çancajada,
mas no li valio todo una nuez foradada.)*
                    (Quatrain 118)

Then Millán prayed to God, was strengthened, and overcame
the devil, whose cries of frustration and defeat are dramatically
placed by Berceo in the first person:

He raised a great dust, a wild whirlwind,
He was badly battered, crying out, "Alas, wretched me!
Always have I heard tell and always it happened to me
'that a bad day dawns for him who has a bad neighbor.'"

*(Levantó un grant polvo, un fiero torbellino,
[fusso] mal crebantada, diziendo "Ay, mesquino!
Siempre oy decir e sobre mi avino,
Que mal dia [l'] amasco al qi a mal vecino.'")*
                    (Quatrain 121)

Millán lived on as victor without vainglory, seeking to keep his
triumph a secret, but without success, for his fame spread. This
inevitably led to visits by people in need of help and of miraculous
cures. Nineteen miracles are performed in the second part of the
book, twenty if we include the encounter with Beelzebub. Millán
makes whole a man whose belly is swollen with humors; cures a
paralytic, casts devils out of those possessed, cures a girl deformed
in her legs since childhood by allowing her to touch his crosier,
since he was in retreat and could not touch her himself.

Later a man who had lost his sight was brought and he, too,
was cured. Then came a devil-possessed priest, and Millán exorcised the devils with a prayer to the Almighty; later two laymen,
one possessed by five demons, were likewise saved when Millán
made the sign of the cross upon their foreheads. Women possessed
by demons were also brought for cure and received it.

A certain senator's house was haunted by a devil which cast
ordure and filth into all food served there. Millán went to that

house, caused its inhabitants to fast for three days, said mass, and then exorcised the devil with holy water. The fiend threw stones at Millán, to no avail, and then quit the city, but not before committing one last atrocity, too vile, wrote Berceo, to relate. His words are graphic and simple: *dezir non vos quiero ca verguença avria* (Quatrain 197).

Hateful people and even devils tried to denigrate the saint with lies and rumors, but without success. Then they decided to set fire to Millán's bed as he slept in it. But as they went toward his bed with lighted faggots, the flames turned back and burned the beards and faces of those who carried them.

More unusual, and certainly homely and practical in the way of miracles, is the following. Men constructing a chapel, sawed a beam too short and were in perplexity. Millán, seeing the difficulty, sent the carpenters off to lunch while he offered up a prayer. How well Berceo closes this little story!

> One of the artisans went to measure the beam
> To see how much short it was, and what length was needed;
> It was restored, even longer than it had been;
> To tell the truth, it was a palm's length too long.
>
> *(Fue un de los maestros la madera medir,*
> *por veer qe menguava, qe avié de complir;*
> *vinoli bien complida, máes que solié venir.*
> *Sobraba bien un palmo por a vos non mentir.)*
>   (Quatrain 234)

When a great horde of poor people came to see him and asked for wine, he performed a miracle and made a small supply of wine sufficient for the multitude. On another occasion, when food was insufficient to feed a crowd, Millán prayed, and a rich man whom he had helped in a previous miracle appeared, bringing more than enough food.

In Millán's old age he was served by a group of pious women. This suggested to the devil that a scandal could be raised and the saint could be accused of fornication, but Millán confounded and banished him. Two monks stole a pack mule which Millán used to carry food to the needy. For this God struck them blind. When they asked Millán for help, he did not give it, but urged them to bear their affliction patiently.

In his hundredth year, Millán learned from God that he would

die. Desiring to do what good he could in his last year, he went to
Cantabria to preach and to save the region from the destruction
which God would send upon it. There a knight spoke harshly to
Millán, who predicted that an enemy army would defeat the people
of the region and that the knight would be the first to die. Of course,
the prophecy came true.

When the hour of Millán's death approached, he spoke to the
brethren, blessed them, and died in the odor of sanctity.

Berceo then describes the saint's entry into heaven. Conducted
by angels, his soul was presented to God. The saints and patriarchs, the prophets and apostles, the martyrs and the virgins, even
Jesus and the Virgin Mary, came to greet him and they seated him
personally. Berceo waxes eloquent:

> The King of Heaven and his glorious Mother
> Gave him a rich throne and a precious crown,
> a marvellous honor in heaven as in earth,
> in which his affair has gone forth in lofty words.

> (*El Rei de los Cielos, e la sue Madre Gloriosa,*
> *dieronli rica siella e corona preciosa,*
> *en cielo e en tierra onra maravellosa,*
> *ont es en altas muevas sobida la sue cosa.*)
>   (Quatrain 308)

God then authorized many cures to be made at Millán's tomb.
So Berceo ends the second part of this *vida* and prepares his
audience for the third and final part:

> We have told you about his precious life,
> until his soul was separated from the flesh;
> but the whole tale is still not finished,
> for his memory was later more glowing.

> (*Contada vos avemos la sue preçiosa vida,*
> *fasta que fue la alma de la carne partida:*
> *mas aún non es toda la istoria complida,*
> *ca fue la sue memoria después más encendida.*)
>   (Quatrain 318)

Miracles took place after San Millán's death, miracles wrought
through his intercession. The first to seek help were two blind men

whose petition is in actuality a short song like those known to have been written for blind men and sung by them. Their prayers were heard and God sent a lamp that burned at Millán's tomb. When, at one time, the oil was exhausted, God replenished it with heavenly oil, which later was used for miraculous healing. An example is given, that of a poor woman whose body was bent, whose feet were dead, and whose vision was clouded. An ointment made from the heavenly oil made her whole.

A certain husband and wife bestowed all their love upon their only daughter. When she sickened, they bore her toward the tomb of St. Millán, but she died on the way. They carried her body, nevertheless, to the saint's tomb, planning to bury her there. But while they took refreshment and rested, St. Millán asked Jesus to restore her to life, which he did.

The train of miracles halts at this stage and we read of how St. Millán gained the sums of money promised to his monastery. He had been dead 360 years when he did so. The people of Spain had sinned, and God had let the Moors best them and exact a tribute of sixty maidens each year. Suddenly there were strange prodigies, hot winds, flames in the sky, etc. Then the Christians, knowing these portents to have been caused by their giving the sixty maidens as tribute, refused to give them again, and the Moors assembled a great army and moved against them.

The Leonese vowed a yearly donation to St. James, Spain's patron saint. The Moors were defeated and withdrew. All Spain made the donations vowed by the leaders. Berceo lists many towns and villages and what each gave, finally remarking that since there were so many, he had forgotten some.

Berceo ends the *vida* by telling people that God gave St. Millán a special gift, that of breaking drouths. Also He placed two small bells above the altar in the chapel where St. Millán's body lay. These bells rang of themselves in times of danger or at the death of great men.

The last quatrain makes Berceo's authorship unquestionable:

> Gonzalo was the name of the one who wrote this tract;
> He was reared from childhood in Upper St. Millán;
> A native of Berceo, where St. Millán was born;
> May God save his soul from the devil's power.

(Gonzalvo fue so nomne qui fizo est tractado,
En Sant Millan de suso fue de ninnez criado,
Natural de Berçeo, ond Sant Millan fue nado:
Dios guarde la su alma del poder del peccado.)
(Quatrain 489)

Typical, then, of the genre of the medieval saint's life is *La Vida de San Millán de la Cogolla;* and yet, originality and a certain personal touch characterize the entire work. This touch, together with Berceo's poetic presentation of his subject, place his first attempt at writing such a *vida* well within the limits of true literature. Few poets have taken a source as dryly presented as the Latin *Vita Beati Aemiliani* and created one as poetic and readable as *La Vida de San Millán.*

CHAPTER 5

La Vida de Santo Domingo de Silos

I Berceo's Art in the Vida

BERCEO'S longest work, containing no less than 777 mono-rhymed quatrains, is *La Vida de Santo Domingo de Silos (Life of St. Dominic of Silos).*[1] As in the case of *La Vida de San Millán de la Cogolla,* the poet used a known source, the Latin prose *Vita Sancti Dominici,* written shortly after St. Dominic's death in 1073, by one Grimaldo, a monk at Silos.[2] Grimaldo's acquaintanceship with his protagonist enabled him to produce a vivid account, even though he departed little from the established and acceptable form of presentation of the typical *vita sancti* carefully studied and scrupulously adhered to by medieval hagiographers. As in *La Vida de San Millán,* Berceo closely followed his source, although Grimaldo had not adhered to the ancient formula of tripartite division for his *vita sancti,* while Berceo did as he Hispanified and versified Grimaldo's original. The reader encounters, then, the familiar division: (1) the saint's birth, childhood, and early life; (2) the series of miracles worked by him while he lived; and (3) those miracles wrought through his intercession after he had died and ascended to heaven.[3] The poets, as was seen in the study of *La Vida de San Millán* in Chapter 4, clearly indicated where each part of his *vida* began and ended and provided definite and facile transitions between the parts.

His reasons for writing this longest of his *vidas* may well have been several, as in the case of San Millán: reasons of propaganda leading toward payment of donations and the attraction of pilgrims to Silos; reasons of piety and dedication to a revered saint; or perhaps to garner favor from God who could reward and protect him. Certainly Berceo gave this last reason in quatrain 4, striking a pious and ingenuous note:

> In the name of God whom we name first,
> Let His be the reward, I shall be His worker,

83

I look forward to a recompense from Him, suffering,
Since for little service He gives a generous reward.

It is possible, also, that he wrote the *vida* at the behest of the
monks of San Millán to substantiate the fact that Santo Domingo
had once been the prior at San Millán.

The poet in his usual fashion maintains a close affinity with his
public. One finds the same techniques as those found in *La Vida
de San Millán:* diminutives common to Berceo's native region,
quaint wordings and syntax, dialogue, ingenuousness, actual or
feigned simplicity and modesty, etc.

As one reads this *vida* and observes its content, techniques,
efforts at establishing sympathy with the public, and general tone,
he is struck with the similarities between it and *La Vida de San
Millán.* The age-old pattern for the medieval *vita sancti,* then, runs
surprisingly true in Berceo's second *vida,* and the poet's strong
proclivity for originality can only be manifest in his poetic handling,
his phraseology, syntax, vocabulary, etc., and the overall "Span-
ishness" of his work. [4]

Following the tripartite plan previously mentioned, Berceo begins the life of Santo Domingo with an invocation (see p. 70
above) and with the mention of the need to write in Spanish. He
ends this section made up of 288 quatrains with lines intended to
hold the reader's attention:

Gentlemen, thanks to God, we have told you
Of what we could know of this holy life;
Hence with God, in Whom we believe, helping us,
We complete this book, and shall begin another.

*(Sennores, Deo graçias, contado vos avemos
De la sancta vida lo que saber podemos,
Desaqui ayudandonos el Dios en qui creemos,
Este libro finamos, en otro contendremos.)*

This is not a model of transition, but it is a clear and frank one,
and is well within the boundaries of good narrative technique.

It will be recalled that the typical saint's life devotes its second
part to miracles worked by the saint while he was alive. Berceo, as
in the case of the life of San Millán, makes this clear in quatrain 289:

We should like to begin another book,
And to make evident some of his miracles,
Which God wished him to do in his lifetime,
In which He should guide us, since we are his troubadour.

(Queremos vos un otro libro comenzar,
Et de los sus miraglos algunos renunzar,
Los que Dios en su vida quiso por él mostrar,
Cuyos ioglares somos, el nos deve guiar.)

Berceo is even more explicit in the transition between the second and third parts. In quatrain 533 he writes at the end of Part II:

Gentlemen and friends, may God be praised for it,
We have finished the second book;
We should like to begin another willingly
So that there may be three books, in one treatise.

(Sennores, e amigos, Dios sea end laudado,
El segundo libriello avemos acabado,
Queremos empezar otro a nuestro grado;
Que sean tres los libros, e uno el dictado.)

He then makes very clear in quatrain 534 the allegorical significance of the tripartite structure.

Just as there are three persons, and one Deity,
Let there be three books, one truth,
Let the book signify the Holy Trinity,
Let the unified material signify the One God.

Part III, again in strict conformity with the pattern of most saints' lives, reveals in quatrain 536 that this final division of his book will relate the miracles wrought by Santo Domingo after his death:

In His holy name, for God is veracity,
And in that of Santo Domingo, the perfect confessor,
We should like to publish in a specific book,
The miracles of the dead saint when he dwelt in heaven.

(En el su sancto nomne, ca es Dios verdadero,
Et de Sancto Domingo confessor derechero,

Renunzar vos queremos en un libro çertero
Los miraglos del muerto de los çielos casero.)

II *The Presentation of the* Vida

Berceo, after making it clear in quatrain 3 that he will present the life of Santo Domingo, begins to narrate a story which will sound familiar to those who have read *La Vida de San Millán,* for much that the two saints experienced as they grew from childhood to manhood is similar. Domingo was a native of Cañas and the son of worthy parents, which did not surprise Berceo, who believed that from noble stock excellent offspring could be expected.

The poet may well have succeeded in endearing the child Domingo to his audience, for he must have been a paragon of virtue:

> He had little interest in laughter or in games,
> And he took little pleasure in those who did;
> Though of tender years, he was serious
> And he was much loved by both children and adults.

> *(De risos, nin de iuegos avie poco cuidado;*
> *A los que lo usaban avieles poco grado.*
> *Maguer de pocos dias, era muy mesurado,*
> *De grandes e de chicos era mucho amado.)*
> (Quatrain 11)

We read of Domingo's boyhood as a shepherd, even as we read of the same vocation in the case of San Millán. This simple, but very important occupation was as pertinent in medieval life as it had been in biblical times, and it is developed and handled carefully by Berceo who no doubt saw in it, even as had Grimaldo, the opportunity offered for winning the interest of a rural audience. Indeed, the poet, seizing upon scriptural examples of young shepherds who attained to greatness, cites Abel, the holy patriarchs, David, and our Lord Jesus himself; and, so as to provide a Spanish precedent, he mentions San Millán, familiar to and beloved by all in Berceo's region. Of shepherds everywhere he wrote:

> Of shepherds we read many fine things,
> For they were prudent, and very holy men:

In many treatises we praise them highly,
Since this profession embodies fine qualities.

(De pastores leemos muchas buenas razones,
Que fueron prudientes, e muy sanctos varones:
Esto bien lo trobamos en muchas de lectiones,
Que trae este ofiçio buenas terminaçiones.)
(Quatrain 28)

Of his own volition Domingo decided to become a cleric, and schooling was arranged for him by his parents. How quaintly human is Berceo's description of the child's instruction, and how revealing, through implication, is the case of the proverbially unwilling student, who unlike Domingo must have hated the classroom!

The little boy came to his school very early in the morning;
Neither his mother nor his sister had to tell him to;
The summer day did not seem long;
The first week passed somewhat quickly.

(Venie a su escuela el infant grant mannana:
Non avie a deçirgelo, nin madre nin hermana;
Non façie dia luenga meridiana;
Anduvo algo aprisa la primera semana.)
(Quatrain 37)

Domingo learned well, became a cleric, lived an ascetic life, and attracted the bishop's attention. He advanced from chanter to reader of the Epistle, and then to preacher. However, after a year and a half the evils of the world appalled him and he feared he would be corrupted by them. To escape, he fled into the wilderness and followed the well-known examples of world-famous hermits, the most famous of whom Berceo lists: John the Baptist, St. Anthony, St. Paul, St. Mary the Egyptian, St. Millán, St. Felix, and the Hermits who dwelt in caves in the deserts of Egypt. Many of these, Berceo tells his audience, could be found in the pages of the *Vitae Patrum (Lives of the Church Fathers)*.

Into the midst of this Berceo injects a most personal touch in quatrain 64, quite unlike what one would expect to find in a *vita sancti,* and worthy of being quoted here to show the poet's skillful use of narrative technique. Grimaldo could never have so per-

sonalized his work.[5] This quatrain is one of the most revealing of
Berceo's attempts at appealing to his audience. Others before him
had called themselves sinners, it is true, and had voiced their *mea
culpa*, but no one so intimately confesses his errors as does this
poet:

> I, wretched sinner, what am I doing in a city?
> I dine well, and I drink well, I am well clothed and well bedded;
> God knows I am not pleased to live in such a way,
> For this kind of life carries with it a frightful outcome.

> (*Yo, pecador mezquino, en poblado, qué fago?*
> *Bien como, e bien bebo, bien visto, e bien yago;*
> *De vevir en tal guisa sabe Dios non me pago,*
> *Ca trahe esta vida un astroso fallago.*)
>   (Quatrain 64)

In fact, Grimaldo's Latin version of Santo Domingo's life, must
have cost Berceo many a pang of disillusionment. He waxes at
times even critical of the Latin source, and though this attitude is
not pertinent to the actual narration of the saint's life, it is most
pertinent to our understanding of Berceo himself and to a compre-
hension of the interesting means he employs to inject his own
feelings of inadequacy into his account, thereby eliciting the sympathy of his public. It is a narrative technique unusual and particular to Berceo. In speaking of Santo Domingo's year and a half as
a hermit, he writes in quatrain 721 in condemnation of those who
didn't know the facts; by "those" he must have meant Grimaldo,
since he was carefully following this writer's account:

> A great piece of negligence occurred among those who knew it,
> That is, the place where he was, since they didn't write it down;
> I suspect that perchance they did not understand,
> That he was always moving about, and therefore they didn't state it.

> (*Cuntió gran negligençia a los que lo sopieron*
> *El logar do estido, que non lo escribieron,*
> *O creo por ventura, que non le entendieron,*
> *Que se cambiaba siempre, ende non lo dixieron.*)

After his stay in the wilderness, Domingo went to San Millán
Monastery to become a monk. There the abbot decided to test

such an exemplary cleric, and he sent him to restore the ruined Monastery of Santa María de Cañas. Through begging he gained food for himself and the brethren with him, and by dint of hard work he rebuilt and expanded the old buildings, repaired the chapel, and bought tools and vestments. Berceo tells us in quatrain 109 that he personally saw the results:

> I Gonzalo, who write this for love of him,
> I saw it, so may I see the face of the Creator,
>
> (*Yo Gonzalo, que fago esto a su amor,*
> *Yo la vi, assí veya la faz del Criador,*)

Domingo, once the monastery at Cañas was restored, was called back to San Millán where he became famous for good works and efficient management as Prior.

Alas, although Berceo writes that it grieves him to relate the matter, King García of Nájera, after winning many Christian victories, slipped into the sin of greed and demanded that San Millán Monastery hand over its treasury.

In what can be regarded as a part of Santo Domingo's life, and at the same time as a brief narrative in itself, we read of Domingo's difficulties with García and of his defiance of the King, even in the face of threats of death. Berceo's audience must have thrilled to this. In a similar fashion had the Cid defied monarchs, as had another epic hero, Bernardo del Carpio. Berceo, cognizant of this, recreates the heated debate between King and Prior for the fascination of the audience:

> You can destroy the body, do ill to the flesh,
> But you hold no power, King, over the soul:
> The Gospel says so, which is to be believed;
> The One who judges souls, He is to be feared.
>
> (*Puedes matar el cuerpo, la carne mal traer,*
> *Mas non as en la alma, ningun poder:*
> *Dizlo el Evangelio, que es bien de creer,*
> *El que las almas iudga, esse es de temer.*)
>   (Quatrain 153)

At last, unable to live near such a monarch, Domingo goes to the kingdom of Ferdinand I who welcomes him and sends him to rebuild another ruined monastery—this time at Silos. There again, Domingo succeeds and Ferdinand arranges matters so that Domingo is made Abbot of Silos Monastery.

One night he has a dream, one which Berceo relates across forty-two quatrains (226–244) and produces thereby, in effect, a second brief narrative interpolated into Domingo's life story. The dream is related by Domingo and is obviously an allegory. He stood on the bank of a wild river and saw two lesser streams, one crystalline, one as red as wine, flowing from the mainstream. Over the river extended a bridge of glass only one palm's breadth wide, at the far end of which stood two saintly beings clothed in white. One held in his hands two jewelled crowns. The other held only one, but it was six times as dazzling as the two combined. They beckoned to Domingo and told him that God set aside the crowns for him. One is a reward for chastity, another for his service to the Virgin for having restored the church and monastery at Cañas. The third, and richest, crown is a reward, also, this time for the work Domingo had done at Silos. At this juncture the two heavenly beings vanished.

After this sequence, the poet inserts, surprisingly enough, an abbreviated biography of Domingo, listing each of the callings and positions he occupied from the time he was a shepherd until he became Abbot of Silos (quatrains 254–258). Mention is also made of him as a visionary and as a prophet.

We read, too, of how Domingo had the bodies of important saints and martyrs buried at Silos. The first section ends with Domingo still alive.

Part II, as is customary in the lives of saints, relates a series of miracles wrought by Domingo while he lived and governed his beloved monastic house at Silos. Each miracle of the thirteen in this part is a brief narrative and is well developed. The first, for example, about the cure of a paralytic woman, requires twenty-four quatrains in the telling. It is well motivated and contains a graphic description of the pitiable affliction suffered by the victim of disease, and offers a very good example of Berceo's narrative techniques:

> A woman from Castro, the town they call Cisneros,
> Whose name was Mary from her earliest days,
> Donned her best garments, took her money with her,
> And set out to market with other companions.

Joyful and in perfect health she went her way:
I do not know whether she went on foot or on horseback;
But she was taken ill in such a fearful way,
That she became as hard as a wooden beam.

She lost the use of both feet, she could not walk,
The fingers of her hands she could not move,
Her eyes were so clouded that she could not see,
Nor did she have control of any of her members.

Her mouth in this altered state
Spoke with a tongue filled with mad words;
Neither her father nor her mother could understand her;
Her friends were filled with annoyance—great, not small.

Since she had ugly eyes, a twisted mouth,
And each arm like a bent twig,
She couldn't go from her hearth to the door,
And all her friends wanted to see her dead.

All those who knew her were disturbed and grieved:
Neither friends nor relatives knew what to do;
A woman entered the home who opined
That the lady would not be cured by hot poultices.

She opined that they should take her to the holy confessor,
A native of Cañas, who dwelt at Silos,
So that when he saw her, he would take pity on her,
And she would gain health from God, our Lord.

This seemed to everybody a very good counsel:
They picked her up and took the road;
At times she turned green, at times waxen,
Since her sufferings were of several sorts.

They bore the poor sick woman to Silos;
She was placed at the door of the confessor;
She seemed more dead than alive;
And people doubted that she would live.

The good confessor, a man of marvelous deeds,
Swiftly and gladly in such matters,
Came quickly out to them from the cloisters,
And told them to come into the house.

He ordered the attendants to see to the men:
They dined on what was there—supper or lunch;
He entered the church to pray to the Creator
To bring health to the paralytic.

He gazed upon the crucifix and said: "Oh Lord!
Who are Emperor of earth and heaven,
Who wed Adam to Eve as wife,
Take Thou pain away from this woman.

"Since she has arrived alive at this house,
Lord, I beg mercy of Thee, that Thou mayest heal her
So that her companions, who are so wretched
May be, on their return, freed from this trouble.

"Let these companions who are in such travail,
Who are confused, sickly, and weary,
Understand Thy grace by which they may be comforted,
And let them praise Thy name, rejoicing and satisfied."

So as to comfort them, the holy man
Cut short his prayer; he wished no long drawn-out one;
He came forth to them, he gave them comfort
With pronouncements of great solace.

"Friends," he said, "let us all pray with all our hearts
To God for the sake of this lady, who lies in such depths,
So that He may return her to sanity, give her her sight,
That she may lose her sorrow, and remain whole."

His cry was heartfelt in all its strength:
He was heard by God; He took delight in it;
She opened her eyes and asked for drink;
It pleased everybody more than a great treasure.

The holy father ordered them to fetch wine;
He told them to heat some of it in a goblet;
He himself blessed it, having poured it into the cup;
He gave it to her to drink in the Name Divine.

The moment it had passed into her mouth
The lady was cured, the pain was dispelled;
She left the bed and quickly made confession,
Saying, "May Thou be praised, Oh Lord, for such a good day!"

> She fell at the feet of the venerable confessor:
> "Sir," she said, "and father, you were born in a happy hour;
> I see that you are well loved by the Creator,
> Since for your service, He is greatly pleased with you.
>
> "I understand, and I know that I am healed through you;
> Through you I have the use of my limbs, my wit, and I have life;
> For this grace from God let me be grateful to you,
> For I know that through your goodness I have risen from my bed."
>   (Quatrains 290–313)

Santo Domingo did not accept her thanks but reminded her that all power comes from God. Only He should receive her praise. He then advised her to go home, avoid sin, and never forget the sickness and insanity that had befallen her.

The story reaches its climax of suspense as the relatives of the diseased woman await tensely the results of Domingo's prayers, the words of which are recorded by the poet. This is typical of the series of miracles related in this second part of the *vida*.

In addition to the miracle just described, the saint exorcises devils, cures blindness, miraculously opens locks to free a prisoner of the Moors, prevents robbers from stealing vegetables from the monastery garden, cures gout, paralyzes a thief, captures Moors, restores a withered hand, ends a famine, heals a leper, and confounds the thievery of pilgrims.

At the end of the second division Domingo dies and is buried at Silos. Part III deals with the twenty-two miracles Santo Domingo performed from heaven, and these, in general, are much shorter than those in the second part and they deal primarily with exorcism. Generally the victim, whether of some physical ailment, blindness for example, or devil-possession, is cured at the saint's tomb. Some are well-developed stories, while others are mere summaries of the events.

The 751st quatrain allows the poet once more to make his public see him as a simple man utterly dependent upon his sources. He makes, at the end of a miracle in which Santo Domingo frees a captive, the following ingenuous admission:

> In what way he escaped I would not know how to say,
> Because the book in which I read it was at fault:
> A section was lost, but it was not my fault,

And it would be great folly to write through guesswork.

De qual guisa salió deçir non lo sabria,
Ca fallesçio el libro en que lo aprendia:
Perdióse un quaderno, mas non por culpa mia,
Escribir aventura seria grant folia.

In quatrain 757 Berceo makes sure to name himself as author, not according to age-old medieval custom which prescribed anonymity to escape vainglory, but rather to assure himself of recognition, it would seem, or because he was obviously proud of his *vida* and wanted to be remembered for it:

I Gonzalo by name, called "of Berceo,"
Reared at San Millán, I am in his grace.
I had a great desire to write this book,
I render thanks to God when I see it finished.

(Yo Gonzalo por nomne, clamado de Berçeo,
De Sant Millán criado en la su merçed seo,
De façer este trabajo ovi muy grant deseo,
Riendo graçias a Dios quando fecho lo veo.)

The second *vida* of Berceo, then, is the equal of the first, and might well have established the poet's reputation as an authority on local saints and as a troubadour of pious subject matter.

Such *vidas* as Berceo's could well have attracted the groups of pilgrims who wandered the roads leading to the many shrines of Spain. Recited skillfully or read with feeling, such poetic *vidas* as those of San Millán and Santo Domingo could have been as attractive as were the secular narratives and epics of an earlier time. In the Age of Faith—and the thirteenth century was an age of faith—the accounts of the lives of holy men and women were as popular as any stories ever told. Berceo's longer saints' lives might have been too extended for continuous recitation or reading, but recited part by part with intermissions they would not have palled upon the listener. The two shorter biographical pieces, to be treated in Chapter 6, might easily have been delivered in their entirety in one brief sitting.

We are fortunate that the *Vida de San Millán de la Cogolla* and the *Vida de Santo Domingo de Silos* have survived. Their rich vocabularies, their wealth of idiomatic and proverbial expressions, their quaint and homely imagery all contribute copiously to the development of the Spanish language and to the unfolding of Spanish literature. Nor can we ignore their extreme importance in the depiction of daily life, custom, folkways and beliefs, as well as to a better understanding of the medieval mind and of medieval poetic art.

CHAPTER 6

La Vida de Santa Oria *and* El Martyrio de San Laurencio

BERCEO'S two shorter biographies of saints, differing to a considerable extent from the saints' lives treated in Chapters 4 and 5, may conveniently and logically be treated in a single chapter.

I La Vida de Santa Oria (The Life of St. Oria)

A. *Presentation of the* Vida

Berceo, in his old age wrote the *Vida de Santa Oria, Virgen.* The second quatrain tells this plainly:

> I wish in my old age, even though I am weary,
> To write in Spanish about this holy virgin,
> So that God through her prayers may be pleased with me,
> And may not take vengeance for my sins.
>
> *(Quiero en mi vegez, maguer que so cansado,*
> *De esta sancta Virgen romanzar su dictado,*
> *Que Dios por el su ruego sea de mi pagado,*
> *E non quiera venganza tomar de mi pecado.)*

In these lines we see evidence again of his desire to personalize his work so as to create an accord with his public.

As in the case of his *Vida de San Millán* and of his *Vida de Santo Domingo,* Berceo followed a Latin source, this time a *vita* written by a certain Munno, or Munnio, Oria's confessor, who set down the facts about her life and visions soon after her death in 1069. This was some two hundred years before Berceo, in his old age, undertook to versify the Latin *vita.*[1] It is a pity that Munno's original has not been discovered since accounts penned by persons contemporary with their subject matter and intimately associated with it always provide valuable and interesting insights and observations. To all intents and purposes, then, the Latin original is lost and its content survives only in two later handlings: Berceo's poetic version, and Fray Prudencio de Sandoval's prose account, the latter published in Madrid in 1601.[2] T. A. Perry believes that Sandoval used only Berceo's *vida* and did not even see Munno's account.[3]

According to Berceo and to Sandoval, the maiden Oria was a native of Villavelayo near Mansilla, six miles from the Monastery of San Millán, Berceo's own favorite and beloved monastic house. She lived from about 1042 to 1069, and Berceo no doubt visited her tomb, which, incidentally, may still be seen by the traveler persistent enough to seek it out. Her parents were García Nunno and Amunna, and they are called by Berceo "noble and important people, holy and virtuous." Apparently they were citizens of substance and possibly of nobility. They endeavored, as loving parents would normally do, to give her a comfortable, and even a luxurious life, all to no avail. Even as a child Oria rejected finery and dressed in sackcloth. She buried herself in books, studied until her eyes were sore, and spent long hours giving alms and persuading her parents to do likewise. But even sackcloth, almsgiving, and fasting were insufficient for Oria, and she entered a convent near the San Millán Monastery and took holy orders. It was while she was becoming famous for piety and good works that she had her famous visions. In the first of these, three well-known saints visited her, Agatha, Eulalia, and Cecilia; they came to her with the tidings that God was grateful for her goodness and that He was preparing an exceptional reward for her in heaven. St. Eulalia presented Oria with a white dove. It flew heavenward, even as Oria perceived an enormous column encircled by a stairway which wound from earth to paradise. Up this stairway the saints conducted her for a brief visit filled with celestial sights.

When Oria awoke from her trance-like vision, she intensified the rigors of her penitential life and suffering, ever hopeful of a speedy return to heaven.

One night as she lay on her inhospitable cot, the Blessed Virgin appeared to her in a vision of indescribable glory, accompanied by heavenly damsels.

One must read this sequence to savor the sweetness of Berceo's description of a vision. His talent for this surpasses his description and relation of miracles. He offers a series of events exquisitely related. The honor of a visit by the Virgin is stressed and developed, and the conversation between Our Lady and Oria is tender and deeply touching. Medieval readers, no matter how steeped in saints' lives, would have found nothing repetitive or ordinary here. The character of Oria is most sympathetically portrayed. Her purity and simple naivete shine forth and endear her to the reader. And the Virgin's grace and love are everpresent. Quatrains 117–138 are well worth the reading, for they exemplify some of Berceo's most elevated and devotional verse. We read in quatrain 118 that eleven months passed after her first vision before she had the second. The vision continues:

> She saw three virgins approaching her in a group:
> All came wearing white robes;
> Never did she see a whiter veil or chemise;
> Neither Genoa or Pisa had such a garment.

> Then within a short while came Holy Mary:
> Joy and delight came to the virgins,
> Since with such a mistress they all had an auspicious day;
> There the entire group was regaled.

> They spoke to Oria: "You who lie in dreams,
> Arise and receive the Glorious Virgin,
> Who is Mother of Christ and daughter and bride;
> Unhappy will you be if you do ought else."

> The nun answered them with great humility:
> "If I could please Her in Her piety,
> If I could approach Her majesty,
> I would fall at Her feet with complete willingness."

> Scarcely had Oria finished speaking,
> When the Virgin went to her. Oh God, what a good meeting!
> The cell blazed with redoubled splendor.
> Fortunate indeed that one who had such a visitor.

> The Blessed Mother, Queen of heaven,
> By far more beautiful than is the dawn,
> Proposed no period of waiting, not even an hour,
> But went directly to embrace the nun.

> Oria drew great delight from this caress:
> She asked Her if she were truly Holy Mary.

"Have no doubt of it," she replied, "my little daughter.
I am that One to Whom you pray night and day."

"I am Holy Mary Whom you love so much,
She Who frees all women from travail:
Daughter, God is with you: if you will persevere,
You will go to a great reward when you die."

All three of the virgins were of equal worth,
All of one quality and of the same age,
Not one surpassed the others in virtue,
All three were equal in every way.

These three virgins brought a handsome bed,
With noble bedclothes, not shabby or mean;
They spoke to Oria who was God's good friend:
"Daughter, harken a little, so will God bless you.

"Arise from the floor which is cold and harsh,
Get into this bed, you will sleep in more comfort,
And be sure that the Queen Who is here,
If She finds you on the floor, will be displeased."

"Ladies," Oria said, "this is not meet:
This bed is for some one old and weak;
I am strong and young enough to endure anything;
If I were to be there in bed, God would be vexed.

"I want a harsh bed with various discomforts;
My flesh does not deserve to lie in such luxuries;
For God's sake, please don't insist upon this;
Such precious things are for noble people."

The virgins laid hold of her, voicing angry cries;
They forced her into that luxurious bedding;
Oria in great resentment, uttered wild moans,
For she was not persuaded to enter all that luxury.

As soon as the nun was placed in that bed,
The cell was illuminated with a vast brightness;
It was filled instantly with a multitude of virgins,
All of whom came to honor the holy recluse.

"Mother," Oria said, "if you are Mary
Of whom the Prophet Isaiah spoke so much,

So as to be perfectly certain, I should like some sign
By which I might be sure that I can gain salvation."

Said the Glorious Virgin: "Oria, my unhappy one,
Who hast been so long encloistered,
I shall give thee a sign, a good and proven sign:
If thou seest the sign, then wilt thou be positive.

"Receive this as a token and a certain proof:
Within a few days thou wilt fall very ill,
Thou wilt be gravely taken with a fatal sickness,
Like nothing thou hast ever seen, but thou wilt receive it as a sign.

"Thou wilt be in great pain, thou wilt be cut down by death;
Thou wilt within a few days be no longer of this world;
Thou wilt go where thou desirest to an honored throne,
The one which Voxmea has kept reserved for you."

Oria lay suffering within her convent:
A great concourse sat outside her cell;
Each one in her chair saying the psalter;
And no one's mouth was halting in its words.

As the sick woman lay in her travail,
She said her prayers, although it was through clenched teeth;
She would have smitten her breast, but there was not time,
Although she tried to lift her hand in token.

The reader is now transported with Oria into a vision of the
Mount of Olives in its heavenly form, not its earthly and actual
state. Its description assumes the pattern of a *locus amoenus* similar
in many of its aspects to the pleasance described in the allegorical
introduction Berceo penned to his *Milagros de Nuestra Señora*.
The reader is made to see, through the dying nun's inner eye, a
heavenly landscape peopled by saints, apostles, and martyrs in
quatrains 139–143:

She was somewhat delirious: since she was gravely ill,
Her vision carried her to the Mount of Olives;
There she beheld sights in the extreme delectable,
And would have thought she was in bliss, had they not awakened her.

. . .   .

She saw a beautiful plain around the mountain,
And in it a mighty plantation of olive trees
Loaded with their fruit beyond all measure:
Men could have sustained themselves here in great abundance.

In the shade she saw a multitude of people
Who all came forward anxious to greet her;
All outfitted with excellent raiment and well shod,
And all would be, at the proper time, ascending to heaven.

These companies were composed of worthy men and women,
And all were clad in snowy mantles;
Their accouterments were like the angels',
Similar to those observed in other ages.

The Spanish is majestic, carrying the action along in a cadence-
like movement possessing the confidence of the poet's complete
conviction that Oria had experienced the vision he reports:

Traspósose un poco, ca era quebrantada,
Fue a Monte Olivete en vision levada,
Vido y tales cosas de que fue saborgada,
Si non la despertasen, cuidó seer folgada.

. . .   .

Vido redor el monte una bella anchura,
En ella de olivos una grant espesura,
Cargados de olivas mucho sobre mesura,
Podria vevir so ellos omne a grant folgura.

Vido por esa sombra muchas gentes venir,
Todas venian gradosas a Oria resçebir,
Todas bien aguisadas de calzar e de vestir,
Querian si fuese tiempo, al çielo la sobir.

Eran estas compannas de preçiosos varones,
Todos vestidos eran de blancos çiclatones,
Semeiaban de angeles todas sus guaniçiones:
Otras tales vidieran en algunas sazones.

It was while Oria was so transported that friends and kinsmen
attempted to arouse her to consciousness, much against her will.
The poet, with considerable skill, reveals her struggle to remain
within her vision so as to avoid a return to mundane and painful

surroundings. One can detect something like despair and a kind of frantic desire to remain in heaven. But it was not to be, and Oria must face again the last moments before death closes in:

At this the sick one was greatly grieved;
She had no desire to awaken at this time,
Since she was in a state of glory in a heavenly locale;
And she was fearful that she could never return to it.

Little pleasure did she show to those who awakened her,
Whether her mother, or the members of her sisterhood;
For she moved in glory among holy personages,
And did not feel one jot of any pain.

She whispered in a weary voice between clenched teeth:
"Oh Mount of Olives, oh Mount of Olives," and nothing more she said;
And no one in the room understood what she meant,
For her words were in no wise clearly uttered.

The good women who sat around her
Observed that she was murmuring, but did not understand.
They regarded it as strange occurrence
And knew not whether she waxed better or worse.

(Con esto la enferma ovo muy grant pesar,
En aquella sazon non querria espertar,
Ca estaba en grant gloria en sabroso logar,
E cuydaba que nunca alla podria tornar.

Aviales poco grado a los despertadores,
Siquiera a la madre, siquiera a los serores,
Ca estaba en grant gloria entre buenos sennores,
Que non sentia un punto de todos los dolores.

Diçia entre los dientes con una voz cansada:
Monte Olivete, monte Olivete, ca non diçia al nada:
Non gelo entendia nadi de la su posada,
Ca non era la voz de tal guisa formada.

Otras buenas mugieres qui çerca li sedien,
Vidian que murmuraba, mas non la entendien:
Por una maravilla esta cosa havien,
Estaban en grant dubda si era mal o bien.)

(Quatrains 145–148)

At length her confessor Munno came, and the nuns called out
his name to Oria, begging her to open her eyes, which she un-
willingly did. How well Berceo depicts the dying woman's sorrow
at leaving heaven and her anxiety to return to it in quatrains
151–152!

> The moment she heard this request,
> Oria quickly opened her eyes and regained consciousness
> And she said, "Wretched me! I was in great glory
> And because they have awakened me, I am in travail.
>
> "If only they had left me alone a little longer,
> They would have done me a great favor. I would have died,
> Since I had already been among such beings
> As make this world seem a nothingness."

Oria then conversed with her confessor and described to him
in detail what and whom she had seen in her heavenly vision
(quatrains 154–159):

> "Friend," she said, "I shall deceive you in no way,
> And I am obliged to grant your request:
> In a vision I was carried to the Mount of Olives;
> I beheld there things that much rejoiced me.
>
> "I saw there a wondrous place, abundantly forested;
> The fruit of the trees was beyond price;
> And there were fields extensive and a world of blossoms
> Whose aromas would heal an invalid.
>
> I saw great throngs of venerable people,
> All well dressed and well shod;
> And all received me with songs of praise,
> And all were in complete accord.
>
> Such was the company, such was the locale:
> A person who dwelt there would see no sorrow;
> Even if one could stay there only a little while,
> He would be able to derive much goodness therefrom."
>
> Munno asked her: "Do you desire to return?"
> Oria answered him: "Verily, more than to live!
> And would you not be able to come with me?"
> Munno replied: "Would that God would permit it!"

Then with the urge to return she tried to get up,
Like a person who desires to begin a journey.
Munno said: "Stay where you are, Oria!
This is not the time to go away."

The Bercean description of Oria's death and interment merits
reading (quatrains 176–183):

Oria's last hour was coming on;
She was suffering more, she was facing the darkness;
She lifted her right hand in a graceful gesture;
She made the sign of the cross, blessing her head.

She lifted both hands, clasping them together,
Like one who renders thanks to the blessed divine King;
The loyal recluse then closed eyes and mouth;
She surrendered her spirit to God, and never suffered pain again.

In her passing she had excellent company:
The good abbot Don Pedro, a person of great tact;
Nuns and recluses, an all-inclusive gathering,
These offered prayers with complete propriety.

Her holy remains were richly attired:
She was richly robed in her order's vestments;
Oft was the psalter recited,
Nor did they leave her until she was buried.

Should you care to know with full certainty
Where this lady of great sanctity lies,
It is in truth in Upper San Millán;
May God for our sakes give her grace and charity.

Close to the church in her sepulchre;
A few steps away in a mountain pass,
Within a cave beneath a hard stone,
Not in such a fine place as she deserved.

The daughter and her mother, both of pious life,
Since they always greatly loved one another,
In death and in all else have not been parted:
Amunna lies interred near Oria.

These are bodies which by right should be adored,
Since for Christ's sake they endured great travail,
May they say many prayers to God
To save our souls and pardon our sins.

In the course of the *vida* we read of two visions which Oria's mother beheld. In the first, Amunna's husband appeared to her to make it known that their daughter would soon die and would definitely be with him in heaven.

In Amunna's second vision, Oria herself appeared—she had, of course, died—and revealed to her mother that she lived happily in heaven among the Holy Innocents.

In quatrains 184–185, only twenty before the ending of the *vida,* Berceo mentions himself and piously seeks God's grace:

They call the versifier Gonzalo,
Who in his labors wrote this book;
May God Our Lord place him in His grace,
So that he may see glory in the Highest Realm!

Although, gentlemen, I should not like to take leave of you,
Although certain details remain to be related,
I should like to complete the work so well begun,
So that there be no one who may embarrass me.

(Gonzalo li dixeron al versificador,
Que en su portaleyo fizo esta labor:
Ponga en él su graçia Dios el nuestro sennor,
Que vea la su gloria en el reyno mayor.

Aun non me queria, sennores, espedir,
Aun fincan cosiellas que vos e de deçir:
La obra comenzada bien la quiero complir,
Que non aya ninguno porque me escarnir.)

The poem ends with a statement revealing Berceo's great trust in his source, which was, it will be recalled, the *vita* written by Munno:

He who wrote this spoke no falsehood,
Because he was a good man of great sanctity;
Well did he know Oria, and he knew her zeal;
In all he said he spoke complete truth.

He knew about Oria, about her mother—all of it;
He was to both a devoted teacher;
May God the great Spiritual Sovereign give us grace,
So that neither here nor beyond may we know sin.

(El que lo escribió non dirá falsedat,
Que omne bueno era de grant sanctidat,
Bien conosçió a Oria, sopo su poridat :
En todo quanto dixo toda verdat.

De ello sopo de Oria, de la madre lo al,
De ambas era elli maestro muy leal,
Dios nos de la gracia el buen Rey Spiritual
Que alla nin aqui nunca veamos mal. Amen.)
(Quatrains 204–205)

B. *Structure and Poetic Handling*

The poetic quality of this *vida* matches that of the two others
Berceo wrote. However, a tone of tenderness is evident in *Santa
Oria* to a degree more pronounced than in his other *vidas*. Berceo
apparently was deeply moved as he wrote of the virgin Oria, even
as had been her confessor Munno, when he set down her story
two centuries earlier.

Berceo's reasons for devoting time in his old age to her saintly
life and amazing visions must have surely been motivated by piety
alone. St. Oria was an obscure saint, not famous for miracles; and
her tomb, which may still be seen, if one knows how to locate it,
did not, insofar as we know, attract pilgrims or those in need of
divine cures. No convent was dedicated to her, as was the case
with St. Dominic of Silos and with San Millán. Therefore, Berceo
did not need to write for propagandistic reasons, as he may have,
it will be recalled, in the case of St. Millán.

It would appear that he accepted the difficult task of composing
a poem about her life out of sheer religious feeling, fearful, perhaps, that she might be forgotten, as indeed she has been in the
onward passage of the centuries. She is not even listed in *A Biographical Dictionary of the Saints,*[4] a very extensive work, among
the six quite obscure St. Aureas therein catalogued. Her obscurity
today is almost complete, and apparently, even though Fray
Prudencio de Sandoval, in the seventeenth century, published a

book about her life, his contemporaries made little of her place in
Spanish sainthood.

Berceo says that he writes her life so that God will be pleased
with him and will forgive his sins (quatrain 2 quoted on p. 96).

He personalizes this *vida*, as was the case in his other *vidas*, but
again to a more marked degree. We read that he felt an urgency
to finish the book. It will be recalled that he admitted that he was
old when he started to write it and adds with very human feelings:

> We have delayed long in the prologue,
> Let us continue the story, this is fitting;
> The days are not long, it will grow dark quickly;
> It is a hard task to write in darkness.

> *(Havemos en el prologo mucho detardado,*
> *Sigamos la estoria, esto es aguisado,*
> *Los dias son non grandes, anocheçerá privado,*
> *Escribir en tiniebra es un mester pesado.)*
> (Quatrain 10)

Santa Oria, like Berceo's other *vidas,* follows the tripartite division needed for unity. There are differences, however, for as the
poet develops the usual pattern employed in saints' lives, he sub-
stitutes visions for miracles. This technique enabled him to produce
a more pleasing and varied structure, for he could thus avoid the
presentation of a series of many miracles, one upon the heels of
the other. In *Santa Oria* he presents only three visions beheld by
Oria, and each is arranged skillfully in diminishing biographical
importance and of ascending spiritual value.

Also the poet has improved the structure of the *vida* in the matter
of the saint's death. Instead of the somewhat awkward coming of
death between two series of miracles, one while the saint lived and
another after her death, as in the case of San Millán and Santo
Domingo, Oria's death actually enhances the unity of the poem.
Her death is predicted in the second vision and is partially revealed
in the vision of the Mount of Olives. When death arrives, it carries
out a didactic purpose and artistically develops the thematic and
structural movement of the poem's second division.

This last of Berceo's *vidas* merits careful study. It can offer a
deep and poignant appeal, even to readers today. In the thirteenth
century of Berceo, and probably in the eleventh when Munno
first set it down, its appeal was strong indeed.

Its very brevity, only 205 quatrains, must have made its reading palatable and would not have wearied the listener.

II El Martyrio de Sant Laurençio (The Martyrdom of St. Lawrence)

The martyrdom of St. Lawrence was a famous subject in the Middle Ages. St. Ambrose himself had written on it in the fourth century. Given the saint's importance as one of the greatest of the Church Fathers and that his works had been copied and recopied and handed down across the centuries, Berceo probably followed Ambrose's account. It is true that the Spaniard, Prudentius, also related the martyrdom of St. Lawrence in his *Peristephanon* (*ca.* 400), but Prudentius also used St. Ambrose's account as his source, and we can safely assume that Ambrose was Berceo's source.[5]

The *Vida de Sant Laurençio,* so poetically presented by Berceo, partakes of two varieties of religious literature. One of these varieties finds its origins ultimately in the *passio* (Jesus' passion on the Cross); the other variety is the *vita sancti* (saint's life), as Curtius so carefully explains.[6] Berceo's *Vida de Sant Laurençio,* is a blend of the two— *passio* and *vita sancti*—although he himself thought of it as a *passio*:[7]

> In the glorious name of the Omnipotent King
> Who makes the sun and the moon to rise in the East,
> I wish to write the passion of St. Lawrence
> In Spanish so that the people can understand it.
>
> *(En el nomne glorioso del Rey omnipotent*
> *Que façe sol e luna naçer en orient,*
> *Quiero fer la passion de sennor Sant Laurent*
> *En romaz que la pueda saber toda la gent.)*
> (Quatrain 1)

What originality Berceo's version of this ancient story has lies in the manner of presentation. Not before Berceo's time had any-one rendered into Spanish verse the famous martyrdom. The poet uses, as was his custom for narrative verse, the *cuaderna vía* described in the sections dealing with his other *vidas.* And, as one would expect, he enlivens the story with his picturesque vocabulary, his quaint dialogue, his use of idiomatic constructions, of dimin-inutives, and his own personal syntactical verse.

Berceo uses the first person, a technique favored by him, probably to establish a feeling of familiarity and harmony with his
audience; and he addresses his public directly, calling them
"friends" and using the second person plural:

> Friends, let us hold this life in little esteem;
> Let us forget the world, let us think about our souls;
> Everything that we forfeit here we shall obtain in heaven;
> Let no fear encumber us, let us trust in God alone.

> *(Amigos esta vida mucho non la preçiemos,*
> *Oblidemos el mundo, de las almas pensemos,*
> *Quanto aqui dessaremos, todo lo cobraremos,*
> *Non nos embargue miedo, en Dios solo fiemos.*
> (Quatrain 30)

Berceo begins the life of St. Lawrence after he is a grown man,
a young cleric, and no mention of childhood is made, another
factor that places this work more in the realm of the *passio* than
of the *vita*. Laurencio and his fellow priest Vincencio have apparently been trained for the priesthood together by Bishop Valerio:

> Vincencio and Laurencio, men without flaw,
> Were both from Huesca, the documents say so;
> Both were Catholics, both of great wisdom,
> Trained by Valerio and of his quality.

> At the time that Valerio occupied the bishopric
> Of Huesca, which was a very noble postion,
> He trained these novitiates; he showed them the way
> To love the Son of the Virgin Mary.

> Both were apt in accepting his counsel,
> As though they had been taught by St. Paul:
> They efficiently carried out their priestly tasks;
> Nor did they pride themselves on the fruits of their benefice.

> They turned all their energies to fulfilling their duties:
> With their preaching they converted sinners;
> With fair hearings they made their judgments;
> Jesus considered them filled with goodness.
> (Quatrains 2–5)

When Pope Sixtus called a conclave of clerics in Rome, Bishop Valerio attended, taking his two young disciples with him. During their stay in the Eternal City, Laurencio and Vincencio were observed by the Pope who saw in their simple Spanish virtue qualities not often seen at the papal court:

> He was delighted with these two priests,
> Because they were as unsophisticated as cloistered monks:
> They spoke with wisdom, they uttered straightforward words:
> And in debates they spoke out strongly.
> (Quatrain 9)

So impressed was he with them that he asked Bishop Valerio to command the two young men to enter the papal ménage—a request which alarmed the Bishop considerably. In his reply one can see just how much the two priests meant to their Bishop, and by implication, how fine they were. This technique employed by Berceo is effective and it lends a certain authoritative quality to the narration. The Bishop speaks in deep alarm and consternation:

> "Well do you understand, Holy Father, since you are wise,
> One of these men is my tongue, the other my counsellor;
> Without them I would hold myself to be poor and in want;
> I would rather have you take from me my bishopric."
>
> *(Bien lo entiendes, padre, ca eres bien membrado,*
> *El uno es mi lengua, el otro mi privado,*
> *Terriame sin ellos por pobre e menguado,*
> *Mas quiero que prendas, sennor, el obispado.)*
> (Quatrain 13)

At length the Bishop and the Pope agreed upon a compromise. The Pope would decide which of the two priests he wanted to serve him. The Bishop would keep the other. The pontiff chose Laurencio, who succeeded even beyond his expectations. Berceo waxes eloquent on Laurencio's rise to prominence. He was a success in every area of his calling—at almsgiving, at the altar, as a confessor, as a counsellor. One quatrain in particular exemplifies the goodness and the service of this young cleric:

> Aside from the Apostles who were of greater excellence,
> Never was the papal court more pleased with any one:

All averred that God had sent him,
And that He should be thanked and praised for it.
(Quatrain 19)

Such glory and esteem, however, did not turn Laurencio's head.
He served all people, ecclesiastical and lay, and he, according to
Berceo, had some foreknowledge of what might come in the future
and he longed for it:

He was a perfect man of extreme discretion:
He carefully attended the troubled, and understood them;
He grieved for souls on the way to perdition;
He longed to be a martyr, to suffer passion for God's sake.
(Quatrain 23)

Then the wheel of fortune turned, according to Berceo's own
words in quatrain 24 *(volviose la rueda),* and the summer of
Laurencio's good fortune became the winter of bad fortune *(Fue
el verano todo en yvierno cambiado).* An emperor more wicked
than Nero rose to power who was also an enemy of Christianity.
In Berceo's words, the evil of this man actually glows like a ma-
lignant and devilish fire. The poet's readers must have been out-
raged, and empathy was surely strong:

The Romans raised up a wicked emperor,
If Nero was very evil, this one was no better:
He was seized with such a hatred for Jesus Christ
That he could not bear to hear His name.

He challenged everyone and all Christendom:
He began to inflict terrible cruelty upon the clergy;
He gave them great suffering mercilessly;
Deliberately he committed infamous deeds.

(Levantaron romanos un mal emperador,
Si Nero fue muy malo, non fue esti meyor,
Cogió con Jesuchristo un tan grant desamor,
De oir el so nomne non avie nul sabor.

Desafió al mundo e a toda la christiandat,
Empezó en los clerigos façer grant crueldat,

> *Dabalis fuertes penas sin nulla piadat,*
> *Façie exiemplos malos de toda voluntat.)*
> (Quatrains 25–26)

Pope Sixtus defended the Church as best he could. His defiance of the Emperor Decius and his punishment herald what was to befall Laurencio. He refused the Emperor's demands that the entire ecclesiastical treasury be turned over to him, and even dared to speak disrespectfully of the pagan gods and their idols:

> "I will sacrifice only to Lord Jesus Christ
> Who made a sacrifice of Himself to save souls;
> I will not serve or adore your idols,
> Which have no life and can give no commands."
>
> *(Yo a don Ihesuchristo quiero sacrificar*
> *Que fizo de si ostia por las almas salvar:*
> *Non quiero a tus idolos servir nin adorar,*
> *Que non an nul sentido nin se pueden mandar.)*
> (Quatrain 44)

For this Pope Sixtus was sentenced to be beheaded. Meanwhile Laurencio foiled the Emperor in another way:

> While Sixtus was in conflict with Decius,
> Laurencio gave all the treasury in his charge
> To the poor, as the commandment requires:
> He dispersed money, he gave to the poor, he did a good work.
> (Quatrain 46)

Nor, while he gave away the money coveted by the Emperor, did he cease his ministration or fail to heal the sick, working miracles as he waited. Berceo gives examples and relates two miracles in which the priest cures a widow subject to excruciating headaches and brings sight to a blind man.

And before Sixtus was executed Laurencio was able to talk to him. Their conversation placed in their mouths by the poet greatly enlivens the narration. Laurencio, cognizant of the Pope's imminent death, longs to accompany him:

"I beseech you, Father, with all my heart,
That you do not desert me, for God's sake and charity's.
If you do not take me with you, Father, in your company,
I shall remain behind like an orphan in his poverty.

"Always when you desired to sacrifice to God,
When you desired to say mass at the altar,
You used to have me with you to assist you.
You should not now, Father, leave me behind.

"If in anything I did, Father, I did harm to you,
When we were together, you must pardon me;
You must not store up any ire against your servant;
Only through this could your soul suffer.

"It would be considered as a great error, Holy Father,
For you to go to supper and for me to be famished.
Master, take me with you: I beg this favor of you;
I should like to precede you in this summons."

(Merçed te pido, padre, de toda voluntat,
Que non me desempares, por Dios e caridat,
Si non me lievas, padre, en tu soçiedat,
Fincaré commo uerfano en toda pobredat.

Siempre quando queries a Dios sacrificar,
Queries la sancta missa deçir en el altar,
Contigo me levabas por a ti ministrar,
Non me devries agora, padre, desemparar.

Si en algo te fiçi, padre, algun pesar,
Quando en esto somos, devriesme perdonar,
Non devries al tu siervo tal ira condesar,
Por esto solo puede la tu alma lazdrar.

Serate, sancto padre, por grant yerro tenido
Tu entrar en tal çena, yo fincar desffamnido:
Sennor, alla me lieva, esta merçed te pido,
Querrie ir delante en esti apellido.)
(Quatrains 64–67)

Laurencio encourages the sentenced Pope with the knowledge
that the treasury is safe and that Decius will never be able to seize

it. Some suspense is injected here into the narration. Berceo's readers
might well have been led to wonder where Laurencio had hidden
the treasure:

"The treasures which I had entrusted to me by you,
Now lie well secured by the grace of Christ;
Decius will not take it from us, for well is it put away;
We shall not lose it, since it has been removed.

"It lies piled up where we shall easily find it,
Nor will it be denied to us and we shall receive it doubled.
Father, do not leave me, let us endure it together,
Let us both, you the master, I the servant, bear up."

The holy bishop spoke to his pious disciple:
"Son, you have said enough, do not be so insistent;
Of much greater worth will be your cloak alone
Than mine, of this I assure you.

"Since I am old and sunken in weakness,
I am traveling very slowly along the way;
But you, as a young man in full vigor,
Can fight for us and gain a greater reward."

(Los tesoros que tovi de ti acomendados,
Con la graçia de Christo bien yaçen recaudados,
Non los trobará Deçio, ca bien son condesados,
Nos non lo perdremos, ca diemoslos mudados.

Alla yaçen alzados, do bien los trobaremos,
Nin nos serán negados, doblados los codremos.
Padre non me desdennes, en uno lo lazdremos,
Tu, sennor, yo tu siervo, muy bien nos conportemos.

Disso el sancto bispo al su levita sancto :
Fijo, assaz as dicho, non me porfiques tanto,
Mucho de mayor preçio a seer el tu manto,
Que non será el nuestro, esto yo te lo canto.

Nos commo somos viejos caidos en flaqueza,
Imos a la façienda a muy grant pereza:
Mas vos commo mançebos de mayor fortaleza,
Podredes combatervos, ganar mayor riqueza.)

(Quatrains 68–71)

The old man goes on to urge Laurencio to accept death when it comes and promises paradise to him:

> "When you take the cup, which they will give you to drink,
> Then will you be with me clothed in a blessed habit;
> You will be well received in the courts of heaven;
> You will see how God honors those who serve him.
>   (Quatrain 73)

After Pope Sixtus was executed, Laurencio was arrested and thrown in prison. There, while awaiting sentence, Laurencio cured a blind prisoner, a miracle which caused a great influx of people suffering from many illnesses and frailties. All were cured by Laurencio.

During this period, Decius summoned Laurencio and told him he must surrender the treasure or die. The cleric's defiance of the Emperor must have warmed the hearts of Berceo's audience:

> Said St. Lawrence to him: "All your threats
> Are more tasty to me than spinach;
> Neither all your henchmen, nor you who beset me,
> Make me more fearful than would ring-neck doves."

> *(Dissoli Sant Laurençio: todas tus amenazas*
> *Mas sabrosas me saben que unas espinazas,*
> *Todos los tus privados, nin tu que me porfazas,*
> *Non me feches mas miedo que palombas torcazas.)*
>   (Quatrain 87)

The Emperor was, of course, furious, but he held his temper. Berceo reveals his opportunist character for he hid his anger, hoping to persuade Laurencio to yield up the treasure. And he appointed Valeriano, the most important member of the Roman Senate, to deal with Laurencio. The priest would not give up the treasure. Instead, he asked for a period a grace, and the Senator believed that he needed such a period for thought. Actually, Laurencio was planning a trick, or at least a subterfuge. Berceo develops this more artfully than does the original work of St. Ambrose:

> "Give me," said Laurencio, "a three-day truce;
> I shall take counsel with my brethren;

I shall reveal treasures to you, since I cannot do so today."
Said Valeriano: "I should expect this from you."

(Dame, disso Laurençio, treguas de tercer dia,
Avre yo mi consejo con la mi cofradria,
Mostrarté los tesoros, ca oy non podria:
Disso Valeriano: de ti esso querria.)   (Quatrain 94)

Berceo seems to relish the subterfuge as must his readers have delighted in it. He builds up suspense and dramatically develops the events leading to the surprise Laurencio has in store for the Emperor and the Senator:

The Duke Valeriano trusted this statement:
He considered that he had everything in his hand;
He praised himself to Decius and did a foolish thing,
For he promised everything to the last mite.

(Creyó esta palabra el duc Valeriano,
Cuidó que lo tenie todo enna su mano,
Alabosse a Deçio, fizo fecho liviano,
Que lo prometió todo fastal peor grano.)   (Quatrain 95)

Then, at the end of the three-day truce, Laurencio appeared before his enemies. With him he brought a multitude of people well calculated to have struck amazement to the authorities. Berceo paints the scene with master strokes and brings it to life with vivid and dramatic utterances:

When the day of the truce's passing arrived,
He [Laurencio] brought a host of poor people—all he could find.
He led them with him, he began to speak:
"These are the treasures God will always esteem.

"These are the treasures which never grow old;
The more they are scattered, the more they always increase;
Those who love these treasures and serve them,
Will gain the kingdom where souls are honored."

(Quando veno el dia de las treguas passar,
Llegó muchos de pobres quantos podio hallar,
Adussolos consigo, empezó de rezar:
Estos tesoros quiso siempre Dios mas amar.

> *Estos son los tesoros que nunqua envegeçen,*
> *Quanto mas se derraman, siempre ellos mas creçen,*
> *Los que a estos aman e a estos offreçen,*
> *Essos avran el reyno do las almas guareçen.)*
> (Quatrains 96–97)

The poem ends *in medias res,* as it were, not by Berceo's design, but because its last quatrains are lost—how many no one can say. The last eight extant quatrains, fortunately, reach a logical dénouement:

> Valerio saw that he was tricked;
> The affair had not come out as he has expected;
> The Emperor was furious and irate;
> He said to him: "How was the matter turned about?"

> They turned upon Laurencio, they could do naught else;
> They said to him: "Either sacrifice to the gods or endure torture,
> For you can in no way escape from this."
> "I will choose to have the torture," he replied.

> *(Vio Valerio que era engannado,*
> *Non li vinie el pleyto commo avie asmado,*
> *Fue el emperador sannoso e irado,*
> *Dissoli, commo era el plyto trastornado?*

> *Tornaron en Laurençio, non pudieron al fer,*
> *Dissieron: O sacrifica, o ve passion prender,*
> *Desto por nulla via non puedes estorçer.*
> *A la passion me quiero, disso él, acoger.)*
> (Quatrains 98–99)

The famous scene of the roasting of St. Lawrence on the grill, long known through St. Ambrose's account, is rendered even more graphically by Berceo:

> So as to give him greater pain and death more horrible,
> They prepared for him a bed made painful in a strange way;
> There were no bedclothes on it nor any wooden part;
> Every part in it was made of iron.

> The ribbing of the bed were slats of iron,
> Set wide apart so that the flames could pass through;

They had him bound to it by his hands as well as his feet,
And then commanded it to be placed in the fire.

They gave him such a bath as you shall hear described:
The evil servitors concentrated upon stirring the fire;
They fanned the flames, giving themselves no respite;
And they delighted Laurencio more than they hurt him.

The flames burned fiercely without containment:
The holy body caught fire in the intense heat;
From the way he was burning, his entrails seethed;
No one who beheld it could contain his outrage.

(Por mas pena li dar, muerte mas sobraçera
Fiçieronli un lecho duro de grant manera,
Non avie en el ropa nin punto de madera,
Todo era de fierro quanto en elli era.

De costiellas de fierro era el lechigal,
Entre si derramadas por el fuego entrar;
Fiçieronli los piedes e las manos atar,
Mandose elli luego en el fuego echar.

Dieronli atal banno qual oydes contar,
Pensaron los ministros malos de atizar,
Avivaron el fuego, non se dieron vagar,
Façienli a Laurençio plaçer mas que pesar.

Las flamas eran vivas ardientes sin mesura,
Ardie el cuerpo sancto de la grant calentura,
De lo que se tostaba firvie la assadura,
Qui tal cosa asmaba non li mengue rencura.)
                    (Quatrains 100–103)

But for the ghastliness and horror of the events one might catch
fleeting glances of humor at the dying man's sardonic words to his
tormentors:

"Please turn me over on the other side," said San Laurencio;
"Look for your best pepper, for I am roasted to a turn;
Plan your lunch, for you have labored much;
And, my sons, may God forgive you, for you have sorely sinned!

"You have afforded me a fine repast, have made me a fine bed;
I am most grateful to you and quite rightly;
Nor would I wish for you a sadder fortune for this;
Nor would I hold more anger, nor have for you a greater animus."

(Pensat, diz Laurençio, tornar del otro lado,
Buscat buena pevrada, ca assaz so assado,
Pensat de almorzar, ca avredes lazdrado:
Fijos, Dios vos perdone, ca feches grant pecado!

Diestesme yantar buena, fiçiestesme buen lecho,
Gradezcovoslo mucho, e fago grant derecho,
Non vos querrie peor por esti vuestro fecho,
Nin tenrrie otra sanna, nin vos avrie despecho.)
                    (Quatrains 104–105)

We have, then, in *El Martyrio de San Laurençio* Berceo's single
effort in the area of the *passio*. His originality, as in his other works,
lies in manner of presentation, personalization, Hispanification,
and clever and winsome turn of phrase, vocabulary, and syntax.

CHAPTER 7

The Shorter Poems

BERCEO, good cleric that he was, composed five shorter pieces whose titles clearly indicate their contents. These are *Del Sacrificio de la Misa (Of the Sacrifice of the Mass)*, *Loores de Nuestra Sennora (Praises of Our Lady)*, *Duelo que Fizo la Virgen (Lament Which the Virgin Made)*, *De los Signos que Aparesçerán Antes del Juicio (Of the Signs Which Will Appear Before Judgment Day)*, and a series of *Hymnos (Hymns)*.

Today it is customary to ask why authors wrote what they wrote and what rapport they might have established with their public, whether it was a reading or a listening public. An attempt has been made to suggest Berceo's reasons for each of his works, and in the present chapter efforts will be made, also, to give the rationale behind his art. When possible, the reasons given by authorities on Berceo have been provided, along with those that I believe to be worthy of consideration.

I Del Sacrificio de la Misa [1]

In the case of *Del Sacrificio de la Misa*, the opinions of other scholars are few.[2] Those who have treated the major works—the *Milagros*, the three *Vidas*, and the *Martyrio*—have had little to say about Berceo's minor poems.

The *Sacrificio de la Misa* is purely doctrinal; it contains no novelesque sequence of events, as was the case with the *Vidas* and the *Martyrio*, and no series of brief narratives in the form of miracles or visions, as is the case of the *Milagros* and the *Vidas*. The *Sacrificio*, the title to be used here for convenience, does not belong to any of the usual genres considered as literature. Instead, it belongs to the area of medieval writings represented by the pious or doctrinal tract or treatise. It is actually a tract in vernacular verse, and in it the reader again sees Berceo's propensity for giving the faithful in Spain, and perhaps particularly in his own special region of Spain, a text in their own tongue where normally such a text would be written in Latin. By and large, the general public did not read Latin, nor did the public understand Latin when it was read aloud. Berceo knew this, as all the clergy surely must have known it; but he, at least, admitted that people did not understand Latin, and with this in mind, he put Latin writings into Spanish—the *Milagros,* the *Vidas,* and the *Martyrio,* as has been stated earlier—and the doctrinal and pious tracts to be treated in this chapter.

In the *Sacrificio* he wrote a clear and attractive personal interpretation of important facts about the Mass, facts which he knew the people did not understand and which he believed they should understand. Indeed, it is quite probable that he had detected ignorance of some of these facts among the priesthood itself. The depth and quality of clerical education and training in medieval times is not something we fully understand today; but from the facts that have been gleaned, it is clear that many of the clergy were ignorant, untutored, and careless as to the significance of the ritual of the Church and, what is even more surprising, unable to read and understand the very language of the Church. The comic or pathetic literary motif of the ignorant monk, nun, or priest is too widely disseminated throughout medieval Latin and vernacular literatures to gainsay the existence of clerical ignorance and lack of education. Berceo himself wrote of this, it will be recalled, in miracle number 3 of *Los Milagros,* "The Cleric and the Flower," and in number 9, "The Ignorant Monk." In both of these tales the cleric cannot read Latin and yet he is, in each case, an ordained priest. Recall that the source of each of these miracles was a Latin book of miracles which Berceo rendered into Spanish, and the reader will realize that at one glance we see clerical ignorance depicted in a Latin and in a Spanish work.

From what we know today, at least insofar as the ignorance of the laity about the significance of the ritual is concerned, one can safely imply that in the Middle Ages, when printed manuals were nonexistent and when so few could read the written word in Latin, or even in their own native vernaculars, an enormous and alarming ignorance was a fact of life.

Priests, overworked in the Middle Ages, no doubt took much for granted, as do the clergy in the twentieth century. Many Roman Catholic laymen today have never received detailed instruction as to the significance of the various aspects of the Mass. In the thirteenth-century milieu of Berceo, the clergy either must have assumed that the parishioners knew what each element of the ritual signified, or, what is worse, the clergy was fully cognizant that parishioners were ignorant of these mysteries and yet took no pains to enlighten them. Not so with Berceo. In the *Sacrificio* he develops, across no less than 297 quatrains in the *mester de clerecía,* a remarkable explanation and interpretation of the Mass and of its origins in the Old Testament. That he couched his interpretation in verse and ornamented it with all of his not inconsiderable literary skills makes this tract a most unusual and compelling document.

David William Foster writes that "One of the most accomplished figural treatments of the mass is Gonzalo de Berceo's *Sacrificio de la Misa,* a unified discussion of the mass as the fulfillment of prophecy. However, because he is dealing with what is already virtually a written document, the 'text' of the mass—Berceo deals basically only with the canon of the unchanging proper of the mass—his poem is more properly a gloss, where his Marian and hagiographical literature is essentially narrative in nature."[3]

But a great deal more than this must be said. The underlying goal of this treatise is tripartite: a description of ritual and doctrine during the period when God imparted to Moses the intricacies of building the Tabernacle with its Holy of Holies, together with His hard and fast commandments as to the kinds and methods and places of sacrifice; an explanation as to the outcome of Old Testament ritual as it changed in the New Testament; and a careful, personalized interpretation of the details in the Mass which were outgrowths of scriptural details. It is remarkable that the poet could accomplish as much of this as he did. His readers, as well as his hearers, would have been well instructed with no more than his interpretation to guide them.

Gonzalo de Berceo's *Del Sacrificio de la Misa* is, in essence, a meditation on the Mass, but it is a meditation with a difference.[4] One would expect a meditation to be devotional in character. Berceo's *Del Sacrificio,* however, is instructive as well. The amazing aspect of the *Del Sacrificio* is precisely this didacticism and its comprehensiveness. In the first part of his work (quatrains 1–16), Berceo gives a history of the Jewish priesthood with all the ritual regulations and accouterments of the temple sacrifices (taken mainly from Exodus: 25 and Leviticus: 16), and then, through Christ's role as priest, he links them with the priesthood of the

Catholic Church and its bloodless sacrifice of the Mass. The theme of Christ's fulfillment of the priesthood of the Old Dispensation is, furthermore, reiterated throughout the work (quatrain 18):

> All the offerings, the Aves and the donations,
> Reveal the meaning of not easily understood commandments;
> All were carried out in Jesus Christ
> Who offered His flesh for the sake of our sins.

> *(Todas estas offrendas, las aves e ganados*
> *Traien significança de oscuros mandados:*
> *Todos en Ihesu-christo hi fueron acabados,*
> *Que offreçió sue carne por los nuestros peccados.)*

In the second part of the work, Berceo, in quatrains 31–59, proceeds through the various parts of the Mass beginning with the Mass of the Catechumens (Introit, Kyrie, Gloria in excelsis, Collect, Epistle, Gospel, Creed). The Mass of the Catechumens is that part of the Mass which those preparing for baptism were permitted to attend. They were ushered out at the end of the Creed. This part of the Mass is treated in rather a straightforward manner:

> The pure vestments which the prelates wear,
> Even the ones which the ordained priests put on,
> All these are representative of the olden times
> And of the flesh of Christ which so well purifies sinners.

> When the sanctified priest appears vested
> And comes forth from the sacristy of the Holy of Holies,
> He represents Sir Christ Who was not understood,
> For if they had understood Him,
>   the traitor would not have betrayed Him

> When the priest beats his breast and cries out *mea culpa,*
> And then kills the doves and slays the animals;
> When he does penitence as is required,
> He stays behind the hanging curtain of the Sancta Sanctorum.

> *(Las vestimentas limpias que visten los perlados,*
> *Sequiere las que viesten los prestes ordenados,*
> *Aquessas representan de los tiempos passados,*
> *E la carne de Christo bien limpia de peccados.*

Quando el sancto preste assoma revestido,
Que exe del sagrario de logar escondido,
A don Christo significa que non fue entendido,
Si non, no lo oviera el traydor vendido.

Quando fiere sus pechos clamase por culpado,
Estonz mata las aves, degüella el ganado,
Quando faz penitençia commo le es mandado,
Iaz tras el sancta sanctorum tras el velo colgado.)
                    (Quatrains 31–33)

The poet explains the various chants, and the reading of the
epistle, and states that:

All this reading is a holy sermon:
It signifies the preaching which
The Apostles did in the early days,
When Christ sent them forth to spread the gospel.

(Toda esa leyenda, es sancto sermon:
Es en significança de la predicaçion
Que fazian los apostolos la primera sazon,
Quando los envió Christo semnar la bendiçion.)
                    (Quatrain 41)

The responses are treated and the signs which the congregation
should make are described:

The congregation rises, each one from his place;
They uncover their heads so as to hear better;
They make the cross upon their foreheads with their thumbs,
On their mouths and breasts, since there should be three signings.

All Christians should make these signs.
While they make them they say these words:
"Thou Jesus Nazarene Who rulest and art strong,
King of the Jews, save Thy servants."

(Levantasse el pueblo cascun de su lugar,
Descubren sus cabezas por meyor escuchar:
Fazen cruz en sus fruentes con el dedo pulgar,
En boca e en pechos, ca tres deben estar.

> *Debe todo christiano fazer estas sennales,*
> *Demientre que las faze dezir palauras tales:*
> *Tu Ihesu Nazareno que puedes e que vales,*
> *Rey de los iudos, salva tus fiuçiales.)*
> (Quatrains 46–47)

It is evident, as Berceo begins to develop his multifaceted theme, swinging pendulum-like from Old Testament to New and back again, that he knew the Scriptures thoroughly. One is not persuaded, however, that the poet always kept before him the actual text of Holy Writ; instead, one surmises that, with full knowledge of the text, Berceo Hispanified and versified the pertinent parts of this knowledge into his inimitable treatise.

A few passages will suffice to illustrate the poet's use of biblical sources and his techniques in presenting his version of these.

After a very brief exordium, Berceo, in his usual fashion, speaks to his audience in the first person and states what he plans to present in his treatise:

> I wish therefore to speak about the Old Testament,
> And of how they sacrificed, and upon which altar;
> Then to turn to the New, so as to proceed properly,
> To place them in accord, to make them harmonize.
>
> *(Del testamiento vieio quiero luego fablar,*
> *E commo sacrificaban, e sobre qual altar,*
> *Desent tornar al nuevo, por ençierto andar,*
> *Acordarlos en uno, fazerlos saludar.)*
> (Quatrain 2)

He then proceeds to give a detailed explanation of sacrifices and sacrificial animals:

> When the Law which Moses received came from
> God's heaven in written and clear form,
> Upon an altar of clay, not of cut stone,
> The Hebrew tribe was to make its sacrifices.
>
> When the leaders who ruled the people,
> Desired to make sacrifice, they offered up a bull;
> They killed goats for the common people;
> A sheep for the priesthood and those in the ministry.

But in the case of the goats they made an exception:
They led two to the temple, such was their commandment;
They beheaded one to satisfy the sacred demands;
They sent the other freely off to the wilderness.

(Quando corrie la ley de Moysén ganada,
Del çielo de Dios mismo escripta e notada,
Sobre altar de tierra, non de piedra labrada,
Fazie sos sacrifiçios la hebrea mesnada.

Quando por los sennores que el pueblo mandaban,
Querien fer sacrifiçio, toro sacrificaban;
Por el pueblo menudo cabrones degolaban,
Carnero por el bispo, e los que ministraban.

Pero en los cabrones fazien departimiento,
Adoçien dos al tiemplo, avien tal mandamiento,
Degolaban el uno por fer su sagramiento,
Enviaban el otro a las sierras al viento.)
                     (Quatrains 3–5)

   The dwelling places of the priesthood are then described carefully:

The house of the priests must be guarded,
In which they were accustomed to sacrifice these animals:
A curtain which was hung there divided it and
Separated the main part of the house from the sacred altar.

The room in front of the curtain was for sacrifice:
There they offered up the goat, the sheep, the bull;
The turtle doves and the pigeons, loaves, silver and gold;
In the part behind the curtain lay a separate treasure.

In the first room was a candelabrum:
It was of pure gold, not of any other material;
It had seven branches, each with its candleholder;
Six were to the sides, one was in the middle.

There stood a table of well-worked copper,
On it twelve loaves of unleavened bread;

No one ate a morsel of it
Except the priests and those who were ordained.

They did not leave the loaves there more than a week:
After a week other loaves were placed there;
The priests considered these loaves as holy,
And when a week ended they removed them.

(La casa de los clerigos avien de aguardar
En qui estos ganados solien sacrificar:
Departiela un velo que solia y colgar
Entre la mayor casa e el sancto altar.

La casa ant el velo essa avien por choro,
Hy offreçien el cabron, e carnero e toro,
Tórtolas e palombas, panes, plata e oro,
En la de tras el velo iazie otro thesoro.

En la primera casa sedie un candelero,
De oro puro era, non de otro madero,
Siete braços avie, quisque con su vasero,
Los sex eran de cuesta, el otro medianero.

Hy sedie una mesa de cobre bien labrada,
En ella XII. panes de farina brutada,
Non comie dellos otri sola una bocaça
Sinon los saçerdotes e la gent ordenada.

Mas de una semana los panes non duraban,
Entrante de la otra otros panes cambiaban,
Los prestes estos panes por sanctos los cataban,
La sammana [sic] passada luego los traslaudaban.)
                         (Quatrains 6–10)

The poet continues with detailed descriptions of the ritual vessels, and other items used in sacrifice, going back directly to Exodus when he sets down the details of Mosaic sacrifices, but he can hardly be said to have paralleled completely that intricate and detailed account. A glance at Chapter 37 in Exodus, an exceedingly complicated set of directions for preparing the Ark of the Covenant, and a comparison of this with Berceo's concise description will illustrate his skill in winnowing out what his audiences could not possibly remember and in supplying them with what was, in his view, sufficient. In quatrains 12–17, Berceo writes what must be regarded as a great simplification of the account in Exodus, free of many unfamiliar objects and of a very considerable amount of detail:

> The ark was all covered with gold,
> Of gold carefully worked by an expert hand;
> It had a seat above it, it was not uncovered,
> A marvelous seat, not lacking in carving.
>
> Upon the seat angels sat opposite one another;
> They covered the entire ark, for they sat with wings outspread;
> They were two and no more, they sat facing;
> They were opposite one another, face to face.
>
> This aforementioned ark was a repository;
> It was filled with the most sacred relics;
> In it were the tablets upon which the Commandments were graven,
> And Aaron's staff, an exceedingly famous item.
>
> A golden vessel, not of decorated clay,
> Filled with divine manna sent down from heaven,
> Which God had provided as food for the Jews;
> It was all stored up in that sacred ark.
>
> Into the holy chamber which lay behind the curtain,
> No one, except the high priest, and once a year,
> Anointed with the blood of a lamb, could enter
> These two sanctuaries about which we have told you.
>
> They name the first one 'Holy,' a familiar name;
> They call it a 'Holy of Holies,' the corner set apart,
> Which lies behind the curtain which was hung there.
> Touching the wine and the water we read.
>
> *(La archa toda era doro bien cubierta,*
> *De oro bien labrada de mano bien dispierta,*
> *Tabla tenie de suso, non estaba abierta,*
> *Tabla maravilosa, non de obra desierta.*
>
> *Sedien sobre la tabla angeles traviesados,*
> *Cubrien toda la archa, ca sedien desalados,*
> *Dos eran ca non plus, sedien bien compassados,*
> *Tenien un contra altro los rostros retornados.*

Reliqario era esta archa nomnada,
De muy sanctas reliquias era muy bien poblada,
Hi estaban las tablas en que la ley fue dada,
La verga de Aaron cosa muy sennalada.

Una olla de oro, non de tierra labrada,
Plena de sancta manna del çielo embiada;
La que a los iudios daba Dios por çenada
En esta sancta archa estaba condesada.

En esta sancta castra que iazia tras el panno
Non estaba ninguno por puerta nin por canno,
Si non el su obispo una vez en el anno
Con sangre de vezerra, si non faria su danno.

Estos dos sanctuarios que avemos contado
Dizel al primero sancta, nomne usado:
Dizen sancta sanctorum al rancon apartado,
Que iazia tras el velo que estaba colgado.)
                    (Quatrains 12–17)

The allegorical significance of the entire sacrificial aspect of the Mass is then presented. The goat sacrificed upon the altar represents Jesus' human flesh (quatrain 19); the spotless lamb is Jesus who was sinless (quatrain 20); the dove signifies Our Lord's simplicity and chastity, the bread His truth and charity (quatrain 21):

All the sacrifices of the First Law
Signify the true Host:
It was Jesus Christ who opened the way
For us to be able to return to the glory seat.

Our priest when he sings the Mass,
And performs the sacrifice upon the holy table—
All this recalls the Host he breaks,
All is there accomplished and there is quickened.

Whether the sacrifices, whether the prophecies
Which Daniel spoke, and which Jeremiah made,
And those of Habakkuk, and those of Isaiah—
All are encompassed in the Cross of the Messiah.

(Todos los sacrifiçios los de la ley primera

Todos significan la hostia verdadera:
Esta fue Ihesu-christo que abrió la carrera
Porque tornar podamos a la sied cabdalera.

El nuestro saçerdot quando la missa canta,
E faze sacrifiçios sobre la mesa sancta,
Todo esto remiembra la hostia que quebranta,
Todo alli se cumpre e alli se callanta.

Siquier los sacrifiçios, sequier las prophecias,
Lo que Daniel dixo, e lo que Iheremias,
E lo que Abacuc, e lo que Ysayas,
Todo se ençierra en la cruz de Messias.)
                    (Quatrains 22–24)

The remainder of the work (quatrains 52–297), deals with the
Mass of the Faithful. This part of the Mass is where the actual
preparation, consecration, and partaking of the elements of the
Eucharist are performed. As one can see, far more elaboration is
given this part of the Mass. No doubt, this is true because the
Mass of the Faithful is more sacred. The Roman Church believes
that the priest or, as Berceo calls him, *el vicario de Christo,* reenacts
the sacrifice of Christ on Calvary and performs the miracle of
transubstantiation. Each prayer, each action, therefore, is, according to Berceo, fraught with religious significance, sometimes
reaching as far back into the history of salvation as the patriarch
Abraham or the priest-king Melchisedeck. The poet intends that
none of his readers should miss the significance of this part of the
liturgy. He explains, for instance, the meaning of the mixture of
wine and water in the chalice at the offertory:

> While the ordained priests chant the offertory,
> The vested priest in his sacred garments,
> Offers at the altar the gifts bestowed:
> The chalice and the Host in place of the animals.

> Let no one imagine that he does so without reason:
> When they pour the water in upon the wine
> An important meaning is involved;
> The priest who does not do it so, commits a great error.

> The wine signifies God Our Lord,

The water signifies sinful mankind;
As these two entities blend into one savor,
So man blends with God in one love.

He who does not wish to mingle the water with the wine,
Separates man from God, and remains a poor wretch;
He commits a mortal sin in grieving the Divine King,
Who for us sinners came incarnate in the Glorious Virgin.

Moreover, when He was crucified on the Cross,
Blood and water flowed from his right side;
He who should wish to separate them would do an ugly thing,
And would not be, through such a deed, pleasing to Christ.

(Mientre que la offrenda cantan los ordenados,
El preste revestido de los pannos sagrados
Offreçe en el altar los dones comendados,
El caliz e la hostia en logar de ganados.

Non lo cuide ninguno que lo faz sin razon
Quando echan la agua sobre la oblaçion,
Ca trae esta vuelta grant significaçion,
Qui assi non lo faze, faze mal ca bien non.

El vino significa a Dios nuestro Sennor,
La agua significa al pueblo pecador
Commo estas dos cosas tornan en un sabor,
Assi torna el omne con Dios en un amor.

Qui non quier volver el agua con el vino,
Parte de Dios al omne, fica pobre mesquino,
Faze muy grant peccado, pesar al Rey divino,
Qui por nos peccadores en la gloriosa vino.

Demas quando estaba en la cruz desbraçado,
Sangne ixio e agua del so diestro costado :
Qui partir los quisiesse farie desaguisado,
E non serie don Christo de tal fecho pagado.)
(Quatrains 59–63)

Berceo, himself a priest, writes *Del Sacrificio* from a sacerdotal
point of view, and he uses most of the ceremonial aspects of the
Mass to instruct his flock. His style reveals the fact that he has

adapted the symbolism for his own purposes. An example of this is found in the explanation concerning the movement of the priest (from the congregation's point of view) from the right-hand or epistle side of the altar to the left-hand or gospel side of the altar after the reading of the epistle:

> Those who do not understand well should make inquiry,
> Why the priest so quickly changes his position.
> He moves from right to left at the holy altar,
> And at the end he goes back where he began.
>
> That right movement which the priest makes
> In his coming signifies the Jews:
> They misunderstood their own Law,
> And for this reason, not their good lives, were they to the right.
>
> The left horn of the altar signifies the Moors [i.e., Gentiles]
> Who have no Law nor sign from God;
> For that reason He gave a special sign to his disciples,
> So that they would not associate with the others.
>
> When the Jews did not wish to receive Him,
> He went to the Gentiles and had them converted;
> They received a gospel which they had not heard before;
> They deserved all the Mass up to the communion.
>
> The tribe of the Jews, born in an unfortunate hour,
> Rejected Christ, because of their sinfulness;
> The Gentiles received Him and were blessed;
> They are His sons, the Jews are his stepsons.
>
> The turning to the right to finish the Mass,
> Shows that when the world is to end
> The Jews will understand their bad way;
> They will believe in Lord Christ who will come to save them.

> *(Los que lo non entienden bien deben preguntar*
> *Porque cambia el clerico tan apriessa logar,*
> *Anda destro siniestro en el sancto altar,*
> *En cabo dó se sovo ali a de tornar.*
>
> *Los iudios significa essa diestra partida,*
> *A la que faz el clerigo la primera venida:*

Essos tienen la ley dellos mal entendida,
Por esso eran diestros, non por la buena vida.

A los moros significa el siniestro cornal,
Que non tienen de Dios nin ley nin su sinal,
Por ent a los disçipulos dió signo speçial
Que non se acostassen a es hospital.

Quando non lo quisieron los diestros reçebir
Passó a los siniestros, fizolos convertir,
Oyeron evangelio que non solien oyr,
E ganaron la missa toda astal somir.

La gent de los iudios en ora mala nados
Repoyaron a Christo por sus malos peccados,
Reçibieronlo moros, fueron bien venturados,
Essos andan por fijos, los otros por andados.

Lo que torna a diestro por la missa acabar
Muestra que quando fuere el mundo a finar
Entendran los iudios todo su mal estar,
Creeran en don Christo que los vino salvar.)
(Quatrains 48–53)

The use of *moros* (Moors) in this context for "Gentiles" gives the work the local and personal aspect which is so characteristic of Berceo's works. Another example which also adds a humorous note is found in quatrain 249:

When the vested priest raises his voice,
Which awakens the people who sit dozing . . .

Berceo's pastoral concern is manifest in his language as well. Especially is it evident when he likens the Church to a family:

Praying to Sir Christ that he bestow his blessing
Upon that family, and upon its offering (quatrain 140);

and in quatrain 65 we read:

The wine becomes blood, the bread flesh,
The family prostrate on the earth will worship them.

The poet also notes the decline in the number of communions, which gave rise to the practice of an enforced annual communion for all the faithful at Easter. Finally he, as many older priests still do when the penitent leaves the confessional, asks his readers to say some paternosters for him.

As the poem progresses, Berceo makes clear to his readers Christ's role in leading mankind back into a state of grace, and as he does so, he reveals that he has been treating the Mass, thus far, as allegory. "That is to say," writes Foster, "the discussion dwells on the present, the New Law, as fulfillment and resolution of a prior order, the Old Law."[5]

> This aforementioned ark was a repository.
> It was filled with the most sacred relics;
> In it were the tablets upon which the commandments were graven,
> And Aaron's staff, an exceedingly famous item.
>
> A golden vessel, not of decorated clay,
> Filled with divine manna sent down from heaven,
> Which God had provided as food for the Jews;
> It was all stored up in that sacred ark.
>
> *(Reliqario era esta archa nomnada,*
> *De muy sanctas reliquias era muy bien poblada,*
> *Hi estaban las tablas en que la ley fue dada,*
> *La verga de Aaron cosa muy sennalada.*
>
> *Una olla de oro, non de tierra labrada*
> *Plena de sancta manna del çielo embiada;*
> *La que a los iudios daba Dios por çenada*
> *En esta sancta archa estaba condesada.)*
>   (Quatrains 14–15)

He tells that Isaiah the Prophet, in Chapter 6 of his book, first recorded the angelic hymn known as the *Sanctus*. He points out the fact that the Mass had its origin in the bloody cross mark made by the Hebrews over their doorways before leaving Egypt. He even mentions the seven petitions of the Lord's Prayer and explains them. As to the first appearance of the *Sanctus* we read:

> Then they sing the *Sanctus* in sign of joyfulness,
> Which the angels sing before God each day;

These hymns of praise we have from the Prophet Isaiah,
Who wrote a noble book of prophecy.

(Desent cantan los sanctos signo de alegria,
Lo que cantan los angeles ante Dios cada dia,
Estas laudes avemos del varon Ysaya,
E fizo un buen libro de la su propheçia.)
(Quatrain 82)

As the *Sacrificio* continues, the poet tells his audience that Christ's passion and sacrifice carry out the fulfillment of the Old Law and, in effect, erase the Old Law (quatrains 24–25). Berceo's readers may have learned in quatrain 28 that, as Foster writes, "The sacrifice of the mass bespeaks not only a relationship between the past and the present but also a more significant relationship between the present and the future, between the church militant and the church triumphant."[6]

When Sir Christ suffered the passion foretold,
He fulfilled the sacrifices of the Old Law;
He elevated the New, silencing the Old;
The Old lies hidden beneath the New.

(Deque sofrió don Christo la passion prophetada,
Cumprió los sacrifiçios los de la ley passada,
Levantó la ley nueva, la vieia callantada,
La vieia so la nueva iaze encortinada.)
(Quatrain 28)

Foster sees in Berceo's *Sacrificio de la Misa* a summary and portrayal of the history of man, of Adam and Everyman. He sees Berceo as dwelling upon "the fall, the redemption and the promise of salvation of man in a way that goes beyond less exegetical descriptions to engage the reader's perception of the panoramic sweep of human experience as it is understood by the Judeo-Christian concept of history, men and events."[7]

The poem is too long and its interpretations are too numerous to be treated in further detail here. Let it suffice to say that it is a personally written exegesis of the Mass, more understandable to thirteenth-century Christians than any Latin tract could have been. If it is as filled with allegory as Foster sees it to be, and as replete with figural interpretations, it is at the same time so presented as

to persuade Berceo's readers or hearers that they have been instructed considerably, and maybe sufficiently, in the mysteries of
the Mass.

The poem draws toward its close with the exhortation to the
faithful that the Mass must not be received by those who are not
in love and charity with their neighbors, and ends with a plea that
the people pray for the writer:

> Thanks to the Creator who wished to guide us,
> Who guides the pilgrims who go to the Holy Land!
> The poem is finished, it is deposited in a safe place.
> We have toiled for days, we wish to rest.
>
> Gentlemen and friends, as many as are here,
> I beg blessing of all of you who have faith,
> That you help me with individual paternosters,
> That you will give me something; you will lose naught by it.
>
> *(Graçias al Criador que nos quiso guiar,*
> *Que guia a los romeros que van en ultra-mar!*
> *El romançe es cumplido, puesto en buen logar:*
> *Dias ha que lazdramos, queremos ir folgar.*
>
> *Sennores e amigos quantos aqui seedes,*
> *Merçet pido a todos por la ley que tenedes*
> *De sendos pater nostres que me vos ayudedes,*
> *A mi faredes algo, vos nada non perdredes.)*
> (Quatrains 296–297)

II Loores de Nuestra Señora

The genres of medieval literature written explicitly in praise of
the Blessed Virgin flourished and reached a peak in thirteenth-
century Spain in the works of Berceo and in the Galician Portuguese
Cantigas de Santa Maria.[8] In the fourteenth century, *loores* (praises)
of Our Lady continued to be written. Juan Ruiz, Archpriest of
Hita, included many in his *Libro de buen amor*[9] and Don Juan
Manuel, of the same century, composed a tract on her assumption
in which *loores* were inserted.[10] Across the ages such praises rang
out, some in poems, some in prose documents and many, too, set
to music.

Inevitably Berceo, who had steeped himself in the ecclesiastical writings of the period, drew upon the vast corpus of the literature of praise and the hymns written in her honor. His own *Loores de Nuestra Señora (Praises of Our Lady)* are deeply colored by earlier praises, set down in Latin and in the vernaculars, and by the considerable body of medieval hymns.

Berceo himself wrote a hymn to the Virgin, although, since no musical notation accompanies it, one could regard it rather as a poem. It will be discussed later in this chapter and in a special section. His *loores* will strike certain familiar chords in the minds of his readers today, just as they must have struck such notes in the thirteenth century. How else could it be? Anyone who wrote in those times, or who writes today in the Virgin's praise must perforce fall back upon the ancient formulas: "full of grace," "Star of the Sea," "Fountain of Piety," "Temple of Christ," etc., if he hopes to gain and hold the sympathetic attention of his reader. Tradition demands it. So it was with Gonzalo de Berceo.

Moved by a fathomless devotion to St. Mary, Berceo pours forth in the *mester de clerecía* a beautiful, devout, and convincing threnody enhanced by his own simple naiveté. The opening lines are a devout and sincere invocation:

> To Thee, Virgin Mother of Piety, I commend myself,
> Who conceivest through the Holy Spirit, a great truth;
> Thou gavest birth to Thy precious son in Thy virginity,
> Serving Thy Spouse with utter loyalty.
>
> In Thy praise, Lady, I should like to be allowed
> To touch the hem of Thy ample skirts,
> Since I do not feel worthy of appearing before Thee,
> So that I will not lose Thy guidance.
>
> With Thy guidance, Lady, I wish to tell
> How God came through Thee to redeem the world.
> Give me, please, a good beginning, give me a good ending,
> So that I may write Thy account.
>
> *(A ti me encomiendo, Virgo, madre de piedat,*
> *Que conçebiste del Spiritu Sancto, e esto es verdat,*
> *Pariste fijo preçioso en tu entegredat,*
> *Serviendo tu esposo con toda lealtat.*
>
> *En tu loor, sennora, querria entender,*

De las tus largas faldas una fimbria tanner :
Ca non me siento digno ante ti paresçer,
Maguer la tu feduza non la puedo perder.

En tu feduza, madre, de ti quiero dezir
Commo vino el mundo Dios por ti redimir,
Tu me da bien empezar, tu me da bien a complir
Que pueda tu materia qual o commo seguir.)
             (Quatrains 1–3)

All the lore of the ages was available to the poet as he sang Our Lady's praises. From the days of creation forward, from the days of the patriarchs, men were cognizant of the Virgin, wrote Berceo:

Patriarchs and prophets all spoke about Thee,
Because they understood Thy virtue through the Holy Spirit:
They all through Thee made prophecies and signs
That they would recover through Thee all those who fell through Adam.

(Patriarchas et profetas todos de ti dissieron,
Ca por Spiritu Sancto tu virtut entendieron :
Profeçias e signos todos por ti fiçieron
Que cobrarian por ti los que en Adan cayeron.)
             (Quatrain 5)

Berceo, as had pious predecessors, saw in Old Testament events hidden symbolisms that represented the Virgin. Sometimes these are surprising and unexpected:

The bush which seemed, to the shepherd, to be on fire,
And remained whole as it had been untouched before,
Signified Thee Who wast incorrupt,
And Who wast not moved from the steadfastness of Thy vow.

(La mata que paresçio al pastor ençendida
Et remanesçió sana como ante tan cumplida,
A ti significaba que non fuisti corrompida,
Nin de la firmedumbre del tu voto movida.)
             (Quatrain 6)

Berceo likens her to Aaron's staff, states that her likeness was in the fleece in Gideon's miracle, that she was the door mentioned by Ezequiel; she was the guide and patroness of Theophilus (recall

Miracle 24 in Berceo's own *Milagros de Nuestra Señora*);[11] and
she saved St. Mary the Egyptian and honored St. Ildefonso. The
poet plays upon his audience's familiarity with biblical events as
well as upon its knowledge of postbiblical saints' lore, a wise and
safe device for establishing the proper vein of affinity. His artistic
play upon the senses produces a delightful synesthesia:

> Mother, Thou wast the stem and Thy Son the blossom
> Which resuscitates the dead with its sweet aroma;
> Salutary to see, quickening to smell,
> Filled with the seven blessings, the sole giver of them all.
>
> *(Madre tu fuisti la verga, el tu fijo la flor,*
> *Que resuçita los muertos con su suave odor,*
> *Saludable por vista, vidable por sabor,*
> *Pleno de los siete dones, solo dellos dador.)*
> (Quatrain 9)

The majority of the 233 quatrains, however, do not treat Our
Lady directly, but rather unfold before the reader's eye a pious
panorama extending from the Garden of Eden to the Resurrection
and Ascension. All of this tapestry, either explicitly or implicitly,
however, is designed to lead the reader's eye to the glorification of
the Virgin Mary. Good Christians were supposed to believe, of
course, that all power comes from God, Who makes it possible
for Our Lady to perform miracles and act as the most successful
intermediary between mortals and the Father and the Son. But
humanity, especially the untutored laity, either forgot this, or simply put it out of mind and regarded the Virgin as a deity indepen-
dent. As human children who have offended their father seek
their mother's protection and, in effect, expect her clemency to
placate their father's anger, so did medieval mankind flee the
wrath of God the Father, seeking the protection of Mary the
Mother. The relationship has not entirely changed to this day. How
difficult it would be for a peasant woman in twentieth-century
Spain to go to God Himself with a small personal problem or even
a serious one of unseemly nature, and how easy to seek the guidance
of the Mother!

Berceo was perfectly conscious of this embarrassment, on humanity's part, before the awesomeness of the Deity. He felt the
same pangs, apparently, and made moving pleas directly to the

Virgin. In quatrains 176 through 179, he describes himself as a
sinner and calls upon her for guidance and protection:

> How will I, a sinner, seem on that Day,
> I, who always did and said vanities and follies?
> I never said or performed a penny's worth of goodness.
> What shall I do, oh wretched me, on that Day?
>
> I listened inattentively to the gospels, I always preferred sin;
> I made myself immeasurably familiar with carnal lusts;
> I never took the trouble to wean myself from wickedness;
> Wretch that I am, how can I appear before Your face?
>
> Badly did I keep the promises I swore,
> Those I had given when I received baptism;
> Always did I strive after what was forbidden;
> Wickedly I did not see such pitfalls.
>
> When I saw how earthly matters flourished,
> And saw vainglory sparkle forth in them,
> With relatives and kinsmen around me,
> I was unaware that I ought to have seen myself in all of it.
>
> *(Yo commo parezré peccador en esse dia,*
> *Que siempre fiçi e dixi vanidat e folia?*
> *De bien nin dixi nin fiçi un dinero valia,*
> *Mezquino peccador, qui faré aquel dia?*
>
> *Oy mal Evangelios, amé siempre locura;*
> *En los viçios carnales entendi sin mesura,*
> *De partirme del mal nunca non ovi cura:*
> *Mezquino commo yré ante la su catadura?*
>
> *Guardé commo desleal la promesa jurada,*
> *La que quando el baptismo resçebi, ovi dada,*
> *Siempre meti en punna en la cosa vedada,*
> *Mezquino non ponia mientes en tal çelada.*
>
> *Quando vedia las cosas del mundo floreçer,*
> *E la su vana gloria en él resplandeçer,*
> *Parientes e amigos redor de mi seer,*
> *Non me membró que en esto me avia de veer.)*

Pious writers in the Middle Ages were accustomed to make

such lists of sins which in their lifetime they had committed, and Berceo's following suit should come as no surprise to his readers. These are after all no more than the general sins of mankind against religion. They would have sounded a familiar note in the minds of Berceo's audience.[12]

But in a way well calculated to gain a closer affinity with his audience, he then mentions in quatrain 180 a sad little personal failing, thereby striking again the human and Bercean note he used so frequently:

> When I was in church the hours there vexed me,
> Empty thoughts caused my mind to wander,
> My brain recalled a host of vanities,
> All of which most evilly beguiled me, a poor sinner.

> (*Quando era en la iglesia las horas me enojaban,*
> *Los pensamientos vanos de seso me sacaban,*
> *Todas vanidades alli me remembraban,*
> *Mezquino peccador tan mal me engannaban.*)

The poet, having pointed out general human frailty, as well as his own personal faults, opens before his audience's eye the terrible plight of those who have failed the Lord. In a series of preachments designed to instill fear, he writes of what happened to those who have gone to hell. In quatrain 185 we hear the damned speaking to one another:

> They will say to one another: "What shall we do, oh wretches?
> Here shall we lie forever, never shall we go forth from here,
> Even though we cry mercy, we shall not be heard:
> What shall we do, miserable ones? Forever we shall live in death."

> (*Dirán unos a otros: Mezquinos¿ que faremos?*
> *Aqui yazremos siempre, nunca de aqui saldremos.*
> *Que clamemos merçed oydos non seremos:*
> *Que faremos mezquinos? siempre en muerte vivremos.*)

Berceo then puts words in the devil's mouth, allowing his reader to feel the fearful impact of his threats to the wicked:

> The devil will reply: "Too late do you remember,
> When you had the power, you did not think;

When you turned yourselves over to me I promised this (punishment);
Now receive all that you earned on earth."

(Respondra el diablo: tardi vos acordastes,
Quando poder aviades esto non lo asmastes,
Yo esto prometia quando mios vos tornastes,
Agora reçebit lo que estonçe ganastes.)
                    (Quatrain 186)

The two quatrains just cited come directly on the heels of a
passage of awful and frightening nature. In the sequence to follow,
we read of the sights to be seen by the good and the wicked on
Judgment Day. Jesus will appear to everyone to reveal his wounds:

Sir Christ will reveal all of His wounds to us,
Which He had, for our sakes, received upon the Cross:
There will all the left-undones be punished;
There will the charities of the good be rewarded.

In what great dread are we to see ourselves!
When we see the blood flowing from His wounds,
We shall see the powers of heaven shaken,
Well should we today fear that Day!

(Mostrarnos ha don Xpo todas sus feridas,
Las quales por nos ovo en la cruz resçebidas:
Todas las negligençias y serán façeridas,
Serán las elemosinas de los buenos gradidas.

En sobeio porfazo nos somos a veer,
Quando veremos la sangre de las plagas correr,
Veremos las vertudes de los çielos tremer,
Debiamos bien agora aquel dia temer.)
                    (Quatrains 172–173)

The poet experimented occasionally in his *Loores de Santa
Maria* in what might be called poetic acrobatics not usually found
in his repertoire. He created, in at least two separate quatrains
(numbers 24 and 97), a species of internal rhyme. Ordinarily, it
will be recalled, his *mester de clerecía* was couched in monorhymed
quatrains. In the two quatrains mentioned, he presents not only

lines rhyming in the final syllable, but within the line at the end of each hemistich.

Quatrain 97, which illustrates this poetic phenomenon follows. Roman letters mark the interior rhymes:

> *Si tu nunca mor*ieses *vivir yo non podria,*
> *Si tu mal non sof*rieses *yo de bien non sabria,*
> *Si tu non deçend*iesses *yo nunqua non subria:*
> *Loado seas Christo, et tu Virgo Maria.*

(If Thou hadst never died, I would not be able to live;
If Thou hadst not suffered sin, I would not recognize goodness;
If Thou hadst not descended, I would never ascend.
Praised be Thee, Christ, and Thee, Virgin Mary.)

The poet directs his praises toward a skillful end, confining himself strictly to the matter of praise. Some of the final quatrains are as beautiful as any Berceo penned, perhaps even more beautiful. Take, for example, number 205:

> The flowers themselves before Your beauty have no worth,
> Since such was the master artist who laid the colors:
> Noble is the handiwork, greater is the virtue,
> Wherefore Thy devotees praise Thee so greatly.

> *(Ante la tu beltat non an preçio las flores,*
> *Ca tal fue el maestro que echó las colores:*
> *Nobles son las fechuras, las virtudes meiores,*
> *Onde te laudan tanto los tus entendedores.)*

Certain concepts of Berceo, simple and yet colored with a deep wisdom and designed to make impact upon his audience, are worthy of note. Quatrains 209–211 are of this sort:

> We can understand this concept in glass,
> How light passes through it without damage;
> Thus didst Thou conceive without any sin,
> As though You experienced it in a vision.

> *(En el vidrio podria asmar esta razon,*
> *Commo lo pasa el rayo del sol sin lesion;*
> *Tu asi engendreste sin nulla corruption,*
> *Commo si te passasses por una vision.)*

Glass, and there is doubt of this, is cold by nature;
But we see heat flow from it:
So it is, when God willed it, it was not impossible
That Thou, being a virgin should bear a child.

(El cristal, non es dubda, frio es por natura;
Pero veemos ende salir la calentura:
Pues quando Dios quisiesse non era desmesura
Que tu, seyendo virgo oviesses criatura.)

We can allot to this another certain reason,
To prove that what we speak is a true statement;
A star sends out its ray and yet remains as it was;
Thou, Virgin, engendered a child in this same way.

(Podemos dar a esto otra razon çertera,
Probar lo que deçimos que es cosa verdadera,
Estrella echa rayo et remanesçe qual era:
Tu engendresti virgo de essa mesma manera.)

Berceo, addressing the Virgin, beseeches Her directly in quatrain 227:

Succor the quick, pray for the dead,
Comfort the sick, convert the erring,
Counsel the wretched, visit the troubled,
Guard the peaceful, pacify the angry.

(Acorri a los vivos, ruega por los passados,
Conforta los enfermos, converti los errados,
Conseia los mezquinos, visita los cuytados,
Conserva los pacificos, reforma los yrados.)

After asking help for Christendom, and especially for his friends and relatives, the poet devotes the last four quatrains to an appeal for his own safety and salvation through her guidance and intercession. Number 232 is of special significance, for it reveals Berceo in his role of a poet whose special mission is to versify the Virgin's praises:

I even beg Your grace for Your troubadour,
Who composed this work, who was Your devotee:
Be for him before Your Son an advocate:

Gain for him charity in the House of God.

(Aun merçed te pido por el tu trobador,
Qui este romançe fizo, fue tu entendedor,
Seas contra tu fijo por elli rogador,
Recabdali limosna en casa del Criador.)

The final quatrain unites all Christian souls in a fervent plea for grace:

Pray for peace, Mother, and for the whole world;
Gain for us salvation and deliver us from evil;
Guide us through this mortal life so that
Finally we obtain the Kingdom of Heaven.

(Ruega por la paz, madre, e por el temporal,
Acabdanos salut, e curianos de mal,
Guyanos en tal guysa por la vida mortal,
Commo en cabo ayamos el regno çelestial.)

III El Duelo que Fizo la Virgen María el Dia
de la Pasion de su Fijo Jesu Christo

In 197 moving quatrains and thirteen unusual couplets to be discussed at the end of this section, Berceo presents to his readers and hearers the events connected with Christendom's most awesome incident—the Crucifixion of Our Lord.[13] In doing so he follows an account written, he avers, by St. Bernard, of whom he speaks whimsically and with an engaging simplicity:

St. Bernard, a good monk and very much a friend of God,
Desired to know the pangs of the complaint of which I speak to you;
But never could he have looked for a better aid
Than the one to whom Gabriel spoke, saying, "God is with Thee."

Not simply once, but instead many times, the devout man,
Shedding living tears in heartfelt grief,
Made the petition to the Glorious Virgin
That She send him Her consolation.

The good man spoke with all his heart:
"Queen of Heaven of highest power
Who shared with the Messiah all secret things,
Be not suspicious in your piety.

"The entire Holy Church will have great gain from it;
Greater humility will appear in Your devotion;
People will have better tidings from Your praise
Than all the masters in France share."

(Sant Bernalt un buen monge de Dios mucho amigo
Quiso saber la coita del duelo que vos digo:
Mas él nunqua podio buscar otro postigo,
Si non a la que disso Gabriel: Dios contigo.

Non una vez ca muchas el devoto varon,
Vertiendo vivas lagrimas de firme corazon
Façie a la Gloriosa esta petiçion,
Que ella enviasse la su consolaçion.

Diçie el omne bueno de toda voluntat:
Reyna de los çielos de grant autoridat,
Con qui partió Messias toda su poridat,
Non sea defeuzado de la tu piedat.

Toda sancta eglesia fará dent grant ganançia,
Abrá maior verguenza ante la tu substançia,
Sabran maiores nuevas de la tu alabançia
Que non renunçian todos los maestros de Françia.)
(Quatrains 3–6)

Berceo allows his audience to view the Virgin as She is constantly beset by Bernard's complaints and pleas, and quaintly he
puts words in Her mouth:

So much did the monk direct his words to Her
That his outcry impinged upon heaven itself.
Holy Mary said: "We must give heed to this,
For this monk never wants to let Us rest!"

(Tanto podió el monge la razon afincar
Que ovo a los çielos el clamor a purar:
Disso Sancta Maria: pensemos de tornar,
Non quiere esti monge darnos ningun vagar.)
(Quatrain 7)

Her only course of action, to stifle his just and pious complaints,
was to meet with him:

The Glorious Virgin descended, She went to the cell
Where the monk was praying with his cowl over his face.
She said: "God keep you, poor tortured soul,
And give you comfort as you voice your plea."

(Desçendió la Gloriosa, vino a la posada
Do oraba el monge la capiella colgada :
Dissoli : Dios te salve, la mi alma lazdrada,
Por a ti dar confuerto e fecha grant llamada.)
(Quatrain 8)

Then follows an amazingly naive and delightful conversation between the monk and Our Lady as Berceo depicts the two in his inimitably warm and human way. What better rapport could be established than providing the poet's audience with such intimate character portrayals as these?

"Lady," said the monk, "if Thou art Mary,
She at Whose breast the Messiah was suckled,
I make my request of Thee, in this confrontation,
Since all my hope is based upon Thee."

"Friar," said the Lady, "doubt nothing:
I am the Lady Mary, the spouse of Joseph.
Your plea brings Me quickly and in deep concern,
For I desire that you and I compose a document."

"Lady," said the monk, "well do I know
That neither grief nor sorrow can touch Thee,
For Thou art in the Glory of God, Our Lord.
Please consider and bring His love to me."

(Duenna, disso el monge: si tu eres Maria,
La que de las tus tetas mamantest a Messia,
Io a ti demandaba, en esso contendia,
Ca toda en ti iaçe la esperanza mia.

Fraire, disso la duenna, non dubdes en la cosa:
Io so donna Maria de Iosep la esposa :
El tu ruego me trae apriessa e cueitosa,
Quiero que compongamos io e tu una prossa.

Sennora, diz el monge: io bien so sabidor
Que toccar non te puede tristiçia nin dolor,
Ca eres en la gloria de Dios nuestro sennor ;
Mas tu busca conseio, fesme esta amor.)
(Quatrains 9–11)

After this follows as surprising and as interesting a piece of writing as was composed in the entire Middle Ages. Probably no one save the poet of La Rioja could have, with so much empathy and simple charm, set it down for a credulous audience. Berceo creates what in modern parlance would be a reporter's interview as Bernard queries Our Lady about the happenings in Jerusalem from Good Friday to Easter Sunday. Perhaps the best device a modern critic or interpreter of this *Duelo* could use to place it before his readers in proper perspective would be to reproduce Berceo's passages in English, at least for enough quatrains to make clear the poet's technique. I have supplied the names of the two— the Virgin and Bernard—so as to depict most strongly their conversation as an interview:

BERNARD: "I beg Thee to tell me right from the beginning
           If Thou wert with Him, when Christ was crucified.
           How didst Thou become aware of it, with what eyes?
           I beseech Thee to tell me, in some way, about it."

MARY: "Friar," said the Lady, "it is for Me a grievous thing
           To renew My sorrow, though I am in Glory;
           My mind has not forgotten it,
           Because I hold it fixed in My heart.

           "No old man, no youth, and no married woman
           Ever suffered such torture nor died in such torment:
           For I was baked and roasted, as though in a fire;
           The agony of Mary could never be weighed."

           (Ruegote que me digas luego de las primeras:
           Quando Christo fo presso si tu con elli eras?
           Tu commo lo catabas, o con quales oieras,
           Ruegote que lo digas por algunas maneras.

           Fradre, disso la duenna: esme cosa pessada
           Refrescar las mis penas, ca so glorificada;
           Pero la mi fetila non la he oblidada,
           Ca en el corazon la tengo bien fincada.

           Nin vieio nin mançebo, nin muger maridada
           Non sufrió tal laçerio nin murió tan lanzdrada,
           Ca io fui biscocha, et fui bisassada:
           La pena de Maria nunqua serie asmada.)
                    (Quatrains 12–14)

Berceo then has her relate in her own words how Jesus was arrested, how the household was confused and terrified, with almost biblical strokes—simple, brief, and packed with feeling:

"On the day of the Last Supper while we were at the table,
And were eating the Body of Our Lord, the sweetest of morsels,
There arose an uproar of armed men
Who burst into the house as though possessed of devils.

"The Shepherd was calm nor did he desert his flock,
But the sheepfold and the sheep were scattered about;
This evil concourse arrested the Lamb,
Guided by the wolf who seized the flock.

"At this uproar which had come upon us suddenly,
My blood froze, I lay dazed:
I wanted to die rather than endure life;
If they had killed me, they would have comforted me."

(El dia de la çena quando fuemos çenados,
Prissiemos Corpus Domini, unos dulçes bocados:
Fizose un roido de peones armados,
Entraron por la casa commo endiablados.

El pastor sovo firme, non dessó la posada,
La grey de los oveias fo toda derramada,
Prisieron al Cordero essa falsa cruzada;
Guiandolos el lobo que priso la soldada.

Con esta sobrevienta que nos era venida,
Perdi toda la sangre, iógui amodorrida:
Querria seer muerta mas que sofrir tal vida:
Si muerta me oviessen, ovieranme guarida.)
(Quatrains 15–17)

The Virgin, when she recovered consciousness, found that the
disciples had fled and that her Son had been taken away. She
clearly records her sentiments and her actions:

"I followed the wolves who were carrying off the Shepherd,
Vilifying them for what they were taking from Me:
They didn't consider My outcries worth three oak-galls,
Since they were taking back manyfold what they had come for."

(Fui en pos los lobos que al pastor levaban,
Reptandolos a firmes porque a mi dessaban:
Ellos por las mis voçes tres agallas non daban,
Ca por lo que vinieran con recabdo tornaban.)
(Quatrain 19)

None of these details, of course, is to be found in Holy Writ,
and much of what Berceo writes here is original with him. She

continues, revealing how She finds Her two sisters and the
Magdalene and how they go as a group to witness the final atroc-
ities against the Lord. She relates then in detail the events as they
unfolded—the stripping away of Jesus' raiment, the flogging, the
mockery by the Roman soldiers, the crown of thorns—and relates
all this to Her own personal reactions:

"They made Him appear in His underclothing
      and stripped off His robe;
All of them as though with one mouth shouted 'baah, baah' at him;
They damaged the Sabbath. Who deserved such a fate
Will be hanged until the seventh hour comes.

"The false traitors gave Him a huge cross;
With harsh whips they laid lashes upon Him;
Streams of blood coursed down his sides,
While I was agonizing with death-like chills.

"That villainous crew did even worse to Him:
They twined thorns around His head;
Placed in His hand a scepter of green cane;
And cried out at Him: 'Hail our King,' which I know He was."

(Pararonlo en bragas, tollieronli la saia,
Todos por una boca li diçien baia baia:
Quebrantaba los sabados: qual mereçió, tal haia:
Será enforcado hasta la siesta caya.

Ficieron grant crueza los falsos desleales,
Dabanli azotadas con asperos dogales,
Corrienli por las cuestas de sangre regaiales,
Lazdraba en comedio io de tiemblas mortales.

Al fezo mas peor esa gent rehertera:
Calcaronli espinas redor de la mollera,
Pusieronli en mano çeptro de canna vera
Diçien: ave rex noster, lo que elli se era.

                    (Quatrains 23–25)

Berceo paints with surprisingly vivid and revealing strokes the
deeper sentiments of Our Lady faced with the sight of Her Son's
disgrace and suffering. Her emotions are laid bare in all their
starkness:

"Never was anyone able to die through extreme grief:
I begged for death, it would not come for Me;

With all My soul I wished not to live;
But the Lord God refused to hear My prayers.

"I, in anguish, was staring at My Son,
Tearing My face, writhing on the ground;
Other good women were making great moan,
Together with My sisters about whom I have told you.

"Our Good Lord was enduring a frightful martyrdom,
Since the Father had sent Him to do so.
He prayed for them, even though He was betrayed,
So that the Lord God would not hold them responsible for the sin."

(Nunqua podie el omne por grant cueita morir :
Io pidia la muerte, non me queria venir,
Io a todo mi grado non queria vevir ;
Mas non queria mi ruego Domni Dios reçibir.

Sufrie el sennor bueno el martirio de grado,
Ca lo habie por esso el padre embiado :
El oraba por ellos maguer que sovierivado,
Que non lis demandase Domni Dios el pacado.

Io mesquina estaba catando mio Fiiuelo,
Batiendo mies massiellas, rastrando por el suelo :
Otras buenas mugeres façient muy grant duelo
Con las mis hermanas que io contarvos suelo.)
       (Quatrains 26–28)

The poignant, personal quality of Her narrative is unequaled
in quatrains 29–30. She realizes that He grieves more for Her, His
mother, than for Himself, and this pierces Her to the quick:

"I looked at Him because He was suffering so much,
And He Who loved Me so greatly, looked at Me:
Amidst all His anguish He did not forget Me,
When I wept, He looked kindly at Me.

"My precious Son, the Lord of great power,
Grieved more for Me than for His own agony;
He accomplished entirely His whole mission
As the Holy Gospel revealed it to us."

(Io cataba a elli porque tanto lazdraba,
E él cataba a mi que tanto me quesaba :
Entre todas las cueitas a mi non oblidaba,
Quando io daba voçes, elli bien me cataba.

El mi Fiio preçioso, sennor de grant imperio,
Mas se dolie de mi que non de su laçerio,
Façie complida-mientre todo su ministerio,
Commo nos lo demuestra el Santo Evangelio.)
(Quatrains 29–30)

Berceo, quite contrary to Scripture, has the Virgin Mary say
that the Jews, unwilling to bloody their hands, gave Jesus over to
the Moors, rather than say Gentiles, for crucifixion, a great dishonor
in medieval Spain when Moors were still anathema.

To make his readers or hearers feel the Virgin's unwillingness
to accept the horrors She saw perpetuated against Her Son, he
causes the Virgin Herself to draw a homely parallel from life:

"I was stunned, I could not speak,
Due to My son's torment I could not be at ease,
For it was a bad morsel, more difficult to swallow,
Than raw dough which is a foul food."

(Estaba estordida, non podia fablar,
Con la rabia del Fiio non podia folgar,
Ca era un mal muesso pesado de tragar,
Mas que la sierva cruda que es un mal maniar.)
(Quatrain 35)

How like Berceo to tell his readers that the Virgin could not
swallow the events of the Crucifixion any more than one could
swallow raw dough!

The poet continues to let his reader see through the Virgin's
eyes and feel through Her feelings. Quatrain 36 is significant in
this way for, in addition, the reader hears Her poignant cry as She
stares up at the Saviour on the cross:

"While the Holy One was on the cross
He cast His sweet glance in every direction:
He saw Me, miserable and sad in great emotion,
Crying, 'Son, Son!' in great despair."

(Estando en la cruz la santa creatura,
Tendió a todas partes la su dulz catadura:
Vio a mi mezquina triste con grant cochura,
Clamando: Fijo, Fijo, a una grant pressura.)

We also feel her fury in quatrain 39 and the outrage of a mother

witnessing a beloved son's death and disgrace and hearing the
reply his tormentors gave to his request for water:

> "When the villains heard this word,
> They who were more rabid than flesh-hungry dogs,
> They opened their huge mouths like mastiffs,
> And they, like evil dogs, offered him a foul drink."

> *(Quando esta palabra udieron los trufanes,*
> *Que sedien mas rabiosos que carniçeros canes,*
> *Abrieron grandes bocas commo unos alanes,*
> *Dieronli mal bebraio commo malos e chanes.)*

The Virgin then suggests to Bernard that they leave this sad
account, since it can all be read in Matthew and in John. She asks
to be allowed to tell of Her grief after Jesus' death. Her words of
sorrow are ringing, living verbal sobs in quatrain 46:

> "Through anguish for My Son, My Father, My master,
> My light, My comfort, My health, My shepherd,
> My life, My counsel, My glory, My sweetness,
> I had neither desire nor savor for living."

> *(Con rabia del mi Fijo, mi padre, mi sennor,*
> *Mi lumne, mi confuerto, mi salut, mi pastor,*
> *Mi vida, mi conseio, mi gloria, mi dulzor,*
> *Nin avia de vida nin cobdiçia nin sabor.)*

She repeats Her own words as She pleads with the pagans *(moros)*
and Jews to kill Her instead of Jesus; She reminisces lengthily
about Jesus' gentleness, His charity, His curing of the sick, His
feeding of the hungry, His forgiveness of the sins of Mary
Magdalene, and His resuscitation of the dead. And as He died,
She repeats, in quatrains 73–76, the words She said to Him, asking
Him not to leave Her:

> "Alas, beloved Son, Lord of Lords,
> I am anguished, You endure the pains;
> Enduring evil treatment by treacherous vassals,
> You suffer the agony, I the foul results!

> "Oh My beloved Son, of supreme piety,
> Why is Your mother kept from You?
> If You would take Me with You, I would be happy,
> For without You I would be not well accompanied.

"Son, I would like to die near You:
I would not like to live without You, My Son;
Son, Lord, and Father, deign to look at Me;
Son, the prayer of a mother should not be disdained.

"Sweet and unhappy Son, temple of charity,
Coffer of wisdom, fountain of piety,
Do not leave Your mother in such society,
Since they recognize neither measure nor goodness."

(Ai Fiio querido, sennor de los sennores!
Io ando dolorida, tu pades los dolores ;
Dante malos serviçios vasallos traydores:
Tu sufres el laçerio, io los malos sabores.

Fiio, el mi querido de piedat granada,
Por qué es la tu Madre de ti desem parada?
Si levarme quisieses seria tu pagada,
Que fincaré sin ti non bien acompannada.

Fiio, çerca de ti querria io finar,
Non querria al sieglo sin mi Fiio tornar:
Fiio Sennor a Padre, denna a mi catar :
Fiio ruego de Madre nol debe rehusar.

Fiio dulz e sombroso, tiemplo de caridat,
Archa de sapiençia, fuente de piedat,
Non desses a tu Madre en tal soçiedat,
Qua non saben conoçer mesura nin bondat.)

And in quatrain 79:

"Son, forget Me not and take Me with Thee:
Only one good friend is left to Me in the world,
John, whom you called My son, weeps here with Me;
I beg You to agree to this plea which I make to Thee."

(Fiio, non me oblides e lievame contigo,
Non me finca en sieglo mas de un buen amigo,
Iuan quem dist por fiio, aqui plora conmigo :
Ruegote quem condones esto que io te digo.)

Like any mother whose son has suffered and died, She recalls
His words of comfort to Her and repeats them in quatrain 31
verbatim, permitting the reader or hearer to listen to what are
purported to be the very words of the Crucified Lord:

"The Lord replied, saying these words:
'Mother, much am I grieved by Your great sorrows;
Your tears and Your outpouring of words move Me
More and embitter Me more than these mortal blows.'"

(Recudió el Sennor, dixo palabras tales:
Madre, mucho me duelo de los tus grandes males,
Muevenme tos lagrimas, los tus dichos capdales,
Mas me amarga esso que los colpes mortales.)

'Mother, You know it all from trustworthy men,
In what way the first parents committed sin,
How the artful devil seduced them,
Uttering lies to them and evil flatteries.'

" 'They lost paradise and lost their lives:
Their entire generation, because of them, was ruined;
The door of the Blessed Garden was quickly closed for them;
And was never opened again until My coming.'"
(Quatrains 83–84)

Mary reveals then how He comforted Her in Her sorrow and encouraged Her to see in it all the divine plan of Salvation for mankind; how He considers Her the greatest of all women, and how He shares with Her the present sorrow and anguish. A very special emotional appeal resounds in quatrain 92:

"Thou and I, My Mother, must savor it:
I enduring the torment, Thou the mighty sorrow;
All peoples must therefore praise Thee
For Thy suffering and Thy Son's for the salvation of souls.'"

The Virgin then tells of Her grief as they took Jesus' body from the cross, anointed it, and buried it in the tomb provided by Joseph of Arimathea. It is in this particular sequence of events that Berceo apparently viewed and studied the bas-relief of Silos Monastery so as to supply the many details he included of the Descent from the Cross. Quatrains 150–152 were included in Chapter 2 on page 25.

The account continues, with Berceo supplying the Virgin's words as She tells about the lowering of Jesus' body from the cross. The details match those of the bas-relief. She bemoans His fate, clasps His right hand, unable to take His left which is still out of Her

reach, and otherwise assist Joseph of Arimathea as the body of the
Lord is lowered from the cross.

We read then the story, as She continues the account of how
the Jews, fearful that the disciples would steal the body and claim
that Jesus had arisen from the dead, asked Pilate for guards and
of how Pilate told them to guard it themselves:

> "Lord [Pilate], you set a guard, since you should do it,
> So that we may not fall into such mockery;
> We would all be better off dead
> Than to be tricked by such vile men.

> "They would make us ridiculous and would write songs about it,
> Since they are unworthy people, recalcitrant servitors;
> They would crowd the whole world—valleys and hills;
> Out of the lie they would make tales and ditties."

> Pilate replied to these jail-keepers,
> For he understood perfectly their characters:
> "You have plenty of guards and doughty soldiers;
> Guard the tomb well, stifle the songs."
>   (Quatrains 170–172)

It is at this juncture that Berceo breaks away from the *cuaderna
vía* of the *mester de clerecía* to insert thirteen lyric couplets.

The quatrain immediately before the *cantica* (chanty) in couplets
whose title, from a phrase repeatedly voiced as a refrain, *eya
velar* (keep watch), introduces this peculiar little *cantica*. The
Virgin, speaking of the guards the Jewish community has placed
before the tomb, says in quatrain 177:

> "Those ruffians sang some chanties
> Which were bitter and very hard for the Mother:
> 'Jews, let us keep watch, let us be alert;
> If not they (the disciples) will make mock of us.'"

The tone and lyric quality of *Eya Velar* can only be savored in
the original and therefore a few stanzas of it must be given here
in the Spanish:

> *Velat aliama de los judios, eya velar,*
> *Que non nos furten el Fijo de Dio, eya velar.*
> *Ca furtarvoslo querran, eya velar:*

Andres a Peidro et Iohan, eya velar.
Non sabedes tanto descanto, eya velar:
Que salgades de so el canto, eya velar.
Todos son ladronçiellos, eya velar:
Que assechan por los pestiellos, eya velar.

('Keep watch, Community of Jews, keep watch!
So that they will not steal from you the Son of God.
For they will want to steal Him from you, keep watch!
Andrew and Peter and John, keep watch!
Nor will you [Christ] know any spell, keep watch!
To come out from beneath the stone [door].
They are all petty thieves, keep watch!
Who spy through the key holes, keep watch!')

No one knows the exact source of *Eya Velar*.[14] That it is a watchman's song is believed, and, indeed, a version in Latin also sung apparently by watchmen has been discovered. Ultimately the source may be folkloristic, even in the Latin version. Berceo either knew the Latin and rendered it into Spanish, or, he knew the Spanish version and simply borrowed it from oral lore or from a written source, and inserted it into the *Duelo*. It is a mere decoration for his poem, but it is a lively lyric piece for which a melody must have been written and one with which we can believe Berceo and his audience might well have been familiar. Its presence in the *Duelo* broke the Virgin's lament and permitted the listener or reader to alter its relentless flow. Also it inflamed the audience to hatred for the Jews who so blasphemed Jesus and His work.

When the Virgin returns to her narration, the audience is prepared for the divine retribution which God visited upon the Jewish guards. Quatrains 191–194 give the entire account of this punishment, but 194 will suffice to present its results:

"Such a terror came upon them and such an evil fortune,
They lost their senses and their wits:
All of them fell dead upon the hard earth;
All of them lay scattered around the sepulchre."

(Vinolis tal espanto e tal mala ventura,
Perdieron el sentido e toda la cordura:
Todos caieron muertos sobre la tierra dura,
Iaçian todos revueltos redor la sepultura.)

The Virgin's account of her sorrows takes on a tone of triumph in the Resurrection:

> "Sir Christ has arisen: Oh God what a great joy!
> Two suns, thank God, came forth on that day:
> Christ was resurrected, and the Virgin Mary
> Changed all her bitter sorrow into happiness."

> *(Resusçitó don Xpto :*
> *Dos soles, Deo graçias, nasçieron essi dia :*
> *Resuçito don Xpto, e la Virgo Maria,*
> *Toda la amargura tornó en alegria.)*
> (Quatrain 196)

The poet takes up the thread of narration and speaks again in the first person. He addresses Our Lady, clothes Her in all the traditional epithets: "lady of the angels," "flower of chastity," "full of grace," etc., and brings the *Duelo* to a close with an invocation in which he begs her guidance, protection, and heavenly grace.

The *Duelo* is as sincere and personal a piece of Bercean writing as can be found among this poet's works. It is, too, one of the most artistic in presentation and in narrative technique, and, as an example of pure emotionalism and of religious fervor it has few, if any, equals in medieval Spanish writing.

IV De los Signos que Aparesçerán ante del Juiçio

Berceo, it will be recalled, had touched on Judgment Day in his *Loores de Nuestra Señora.* Like the majority of believers in his century, he trembled at the thought of it and he considered it necessary to personalize and popularize (in the better connotations of the word) that time of dread. Those who could read Latin, a group made up almost exclusively of the clergy, could peruse St. Jerome's writings about Judgment Day. Berceo, indeed, states in his first quatrain that he will repeat to his audience a "sermon" taken from a holy treatise written by Jerome who had, in his own time, borrowed from Hebrew documents. St. Jerome learned grim facts:

> Gentlemen, if you should care to listen briefly,
> I should like to discourse for a short time

On a tract which was taken from a holy writing,
Which St. Jerome, an invaluable primate, wrote.

Father Jerome, a shepherd who should be understood by us,
Reading in Hebrew that same tract,
Came upon startling matters in a strange document;
Let him who wishes to hear them have a good lunch.

The good man found out among all the rest
That before judgment, that is, final judgment,
Very great signs will appear, a dreadful period,
In which the world will be seen in mortal straits.

Therefore this competent man wrote
So that the people who wandered in sin should be fearful;
So that they would improve their ways, would please God;
So that by Christ they will not be deserted.

(Sennores, si quisieredes attender un poquiello,
Querriavos contar un poco de ratiello
Un sermon que fue priso de un sancto libriello
Que fizo Sant Iheronimo un preçioso cabdiello.

Nuestro padre Iheronimo pastor de nos entienda,
Leyendo en ebreo en essa su leyenda
Trovó cosas estrannas de estranna façienda:
Qui las oyr quisiere, tenga que bien merienda.

Trovó el omne bueno entre todo lo al
Que ante del juiçio cabdal,
Vernan muy grandes signos, un fiero temporal,
Que se verá el mundo en pressura mortal.

Por esso lo escribió el varon acordado,
Que se tema el pueblo que anda desviado,
Meiore en costumbres, faga a Dios pagado,
Que non sea de Xpo estonçe desemparado.)
(Quatrains 1–4)

The poet then proceeds to list some of the signs and portents which were to make themselves apparent, according to St. Jerome:

This will be one of the strange signs:
The sea will mount over many areas up to the heavens,
Higher far than the mountains and higher than the hills,
So that fishes will find themselves on dry ground.

But the sea will be very solid in its entirety,
It will not be able to level itself, it will be like ice,
Like a hillock raised up, or a wall of masonry;
All who see it will be badly frightened.

(Esti será el uno de los signos dubdados :
Subirá a las nubes el mar muchos estados,
Mas alto que las sierras e mas que los collados,
Tanto que en sequero fincarán los pescados.

Pero en su derecha será el muy quedado,
Non podrá estenderse, será commo elado,
Commo parés enfiesta o muro bien labrado,
Quiquiera que lo vea, será mal espantado.)
(Quatrains 5–6)

Day by day the portents are described as they will appear:

On the second day all will be submerged
Lower than the earth, as though pushed downward;
No man will consider even to look at it;
But it will quickly be returned to its normal state.

It is fitting to speak about the third portent,
Which will be a frightful thing and a terrible blow:
Fishes will pass over the entire sea,
Uttering loud cries, unable to be still.

The birds also, both the small and the large,
All quite terrified will fly about screaming;
So, too, the beasts, both wild and domestic;
Nor will they be able to return to their lairs.
(Quatrains 7–9)

Terrible events and signs will be manifest for fourteen days and nights. On the fifth day even plant life on the planet will offer portents:

On the fifth day the portents will be fearful:
From all herbs and trees and verdure,
According to St. Jerome, will drip pure blood;
Those who do not see it will be the lucky ones.
(Quatrain 11)

Worse still is to be found in quatrains 14–16:

Men with anguish and in grief and with this terror,
From these portents of so frightful a form,
Will look for any corner in which to hide themselves.
They will say: "Mountains, cover us, for we are in trouble."

On the eighth day another horror will come about:
The whole earth will shake in a terrible manner;
No living thing in the world will stay on its feet;
Nothing will be so steady that it won't fall down.

On the ninth day other portents will befall:
The mountain ranges and all the hills will lie flat;
Hills and valleys will be as companions;
All—both highways and bypaths—will be alike.

Berceo lightens the final blow by painting in quatrain 22 an image, somehow both pitiable and ludicrous, of mankind scuttling to answer the angel's trumpet:[15]

On the final day as the Prophet says,
The angelic herald will sound his trumpet;
Each of the dead in his shroud will hear it;
And they will run to Judgment each with his valise.

(El dia postrimero commo diçe el Propheta,
El angel pregonero sonará la corneta,
Oyrlo an los muertos cada uno en su capseta,
Correrán al juiçio quisque con su maleta.)

The hordes of the risen dead embody all ages and classes of people. The poet waxes almost macabre as he discusses the details of Resurrection:

All who were ever born and were begotten,
As many souls as there were which were quickened,
Whether the birds ate their bodies or whether they were scattered
    to the wind,
All on that day will be assembled there.

All who died no matter at what age,
Children or middle aged or extreme old age,
All those of thirty years, the tally of the Trinity,
Will come on that day before God's Majesty.

(Quantos nunca nasçieron e fueron engendrados,
Quantos almas ovieron e fueron vivificados,

Si los comieron aves ó fueron ablentados,
Todos en aquel dia alli serán juntados.

Quantos nunca murieron en qualquiera edat,
Ninnos o eguados o en grant vegedat,
Todos de treinta annos, cuento de trinidat,
Vernan en essi dia ante la magestat.)
(Quatrains 23–24)

The scene of Judgment is succinctly painted in quatrain 25:

The just will be stationed on the right hand;
The wicked, an unmeasurable horde, at the left;
The King will be in the midst with His retinue resplendent,
Close to the Glorious Virgin, replete with charity.

We read of the praise Jesus heaps upon the pious and see in the
poet's words how he could have impressed his readers, leading
them to ponder the value of good works as he reveals their reward
in heaven:

The Glorious King will then turn to the just;
He will direct to them a sermon tempered and gratifying:
"Come, you blessed ones, who are precious to My Father,
Accept My eternal and delightful rule.

"Receive the reward for all you did to serve Me:
For when I hungered, well did you nourish Me;
You saw Me thirsty, much did you give Me to drink;
If I needed clothing, willingly you clothed Me.

"When I sought shelter at your door,
Immediately you gave it to Me with cheerful good will;
In the travail I suffered, I found in you a refuge;
To you all I now shall make a payment.

"For all you did for Me you will have a good reward:
You will rule with Me through all the ages;
You will live in great glory, never will you know sorrow;
You will sing forever heavenly choruses before Me."

(Tornarse a los justos ha el Rey glorioso,
Façerlis a un sermon temprado e sabroso:
Venit los benedictos del mi padre preçioso,
Resçebit el mi regno largo e deliçioso.

Resçebit galardon de lo que me serviestes,
Ca quando ove fambre, vos bien me apaçiestes,
Vidiestesme sediento, bien a beber me diestes,
Si me menguó vestido, de grado me vestiestes.

Quando a vuestras puertas demandaba posada,
Vos luego me la diestes con voluntat pagada:
En las cuitas que ovi, fallé en vos entrada:
Quierovos yo agora de todo dar soldada.

De lo que me serviestes buen gualardon abredes,
Por seculorum secula conmigo regnaredes,
Vivredes en grant gloria, nunca pesar avredes,
Siempre laudes angelicas ante mi cantaredes.)
(Quatrains 27–30)

Then in fury—for we read fury in His stern confrontation with them—Jesus addresses the wicked:

He will turn to the left, angry and irate,
He will give them a harsh command as tidings:
"Begone, evil minions of wickedness,
Begone with your master, your champion.

"Go to burn in the fire which is akindled
For you and Lucifer and all his host;
You will have no succor, this is determined;
According to the master you served will be your reward."

(Tornará a siniestro sannoso e irado,
Deçirles a por nuevas un esquivo mandado:
Ydvos maldictos ministros del peccado,
Yt con vuestro maestro, vuestro adelantado.

Yt arder en el fuego que está avivado
Para vos e a Luçifer e a todo su fonsado:
Acorro non avredes, esto es delibrado:
A qual sennor serviestes reçibredes tal dado.)
(Quatrains 31–32)

Then, lest the wicked see injustice in His judgment, Jesus explains His reasons for the punishments He allocates and justifies His sternness:

"When I was famished, when I was miserable,
You would not give Me heed, nor would offer Me a morsel;
When I had great thirst, you gave Me no thought;
And well did you manage not to give Me shelter.

"If you had given Me even one thing,
I would certainly have kept it set by for you.
Indeed, you were so vile that you gave Me nothing,
Nor am I unmindful of your doings.

"When some poor man came to your door,
In wretched rags, beseeching you in My name,
You would give him neither bread nor wine;
Today, if you had cared for him, he would be your sponsor."

(Quando fambre avia, andaba muy lazdrado,
Oyrme non quisiestes, nin darme un bocado;
Si io grant set avia non aviades cuidado,
E muy bien vos guardastes de darme hospedado.

Si vos alguna cosa me oviesedes dada,
Yo bien vos la ternia agora condessada;
Mas fuestes tan cruos que non me diestes nada:
Io la vuestra crueza non la e olvidada!

Quando el pobreçiello a vuestra puerta vino
Pediendo en mi nombre con habito mezquino,
Vos dar non le quisiestes nin del pan nin del vino:
Oi, si vos dél pensassedes, él vos seria padrino.)
(Quatrains 33–35)

Hell's torments must have fascinated Berceo, perhaps even more
than heaven's rewards, for he dwells upon the former, especially
in quatrains 36–40:

"Ready will be the angels, the hellish angels,
With lighted torches and strong whips,
To drive the wicked before them with deadly lashes;
May Jesus Christ protect us from such servitors.

"They will take them to the fire, to the fire infernal,
Where never will they see light, but only care and evil;
They will clothe them in sundry robes of abrasive sackcloth,
Which will scratch each one a good amount.

"They will suffer hunger and cold, shivering and sweating;
Heat mingled with cold immeasurably, fierce thirst;
Within their hearts they will have a great burning;
Those who refused to believe the Holy Scripture.

"Upon them will feed serpents and scorpions
Which have horrid fangs and sharp stingers;
These will press their jaws against their hearts;
Never will they in any season find remedy.

"They will provide them with nasty suppers and worse lunches;
Much smoke in their eyes, a great fetor in their nostrils;
Vinegar on the lips, bile on the palate;
Flames in the throat, spasms in the loins."

(Pressos serán los angeles, angeles infernales,
Con candelas ardientes e con fuertes dogales
Coger los an delante con azotes mortales,
Ihu Xpo nos guarde de tales serviçiales.

Levarlos an al fuego, al fuego infernal,
Do nunca verán lumbre, sinon cuyta e mal,
Darlis an sendas saias de un aspero sayal,
Que cada una dellas pesará un quintal.

Averán fambre e frio, temblor e callentura,
Ardor vuelto con frio, set fiera sin mesura,
Entre sus corazones averan muy grant ardura,
Que creer non quisieron la sancta Scriptura.

Comerlos an serpientes e los escorpiones
Que an amargos dientes, agudos aguijones:
Meterlis an los rostros fasta los corazones,
Nunca abrán remedio en ningunas sazones.

Darlis an malas çenas et peores yantares,
Grant fumo a los oios, grant fedor a las nares,
Vinagre a los labros, fiel a los paladares,
Fuego a las gargantas, torzon a los yjares.)

In effect, then, Berceo, through St. Jerome's work, but also through his own colorful Hispanification of Jerome's ideology and imagery, creates in Spanish an almost Dantesque *Inferno*. As, like

Dante a century later, and like Jerome so many years before, Berceo classifies the sinners suffering in hell and purgatory, he dwells upon their punishments, and with detailed descriptions of their torments; he paints a hideous picture well calculated to instill dread in his audience, well calculated to frighten the sinner back into the paths of righteousness. With vigor and enthusiasm the poet wrote the following quatrain, number 41:

> They will hang the evil-doers by their tongues,
> And those who bear false witness, and those who mock;
> They will pardon neither kings nor emperors;
> According to their rule as masters, so shall they be servants.

> *(Colgarán de las lenguas los escatimadores,*
> *Los que testiguan falso, e los escarnidores;*
> *Non perdonarán a reyes nin a emperadores,*
> *Avran tales servientes quales fueron sennores.)*

The last couplet of this quatrain is reminiscent of the Dance of Death, in which all classes are leveled, in which no living soul escapes.

We read then of a various group of sinners: the rich (quatrain 42), the false servitors (quatrain 43), the clergy who live like secular men (quatrain 44), the proud and haughty, the evil judges (quatrain 45), and the envious (quatrain 46). Each group is described and characterized and disparaged by Berceo.

Then, like a ray of sunlight in a day of gloom the poet speaks of happier matters:

> Let us change the subject, let us turn to another;
> Let us not dwell longer upon distasteful matters;
> Let us turn to the good company of the righteous;
> Let us versify the blessings for which we may hope.

> *(Cambiemos la materia, en otro son tornemos,*
> *En razon dessabrida mucho non detardemos,*
> *A la buenna companna de los justos tornemos,*
> *El bien que esperamos esso versifiquemos.)*
> (Quatrain 48)

Triumphantly, colorfully, enthusiastically, the poet depicts for the blessed the brilliant pageantry and pomp of Jesus' entry into the high court of God. If he wrote with purpose, and perhaps with a certain relish, about the punishment of the wicked—and indeed he did—then he wrote with even greater pleasure of the rewards of the good.

Pomp and ceremony, colorful processions, marching hosts, choirs of singers, and spectacle in general were dear to medieval man. Berceo presented pure spectacle to his audience as he wrote quatrains 49–51:

> The King of Kings, the Righteous Governor,
> Who sets up the order of things with any counsellor,
> With His rich procession, and leading it Himself,
> Will enter into the glory of the True Father.

> The precious company, consecrated by Christ,
> Blessed by the Father, summoned by the Son,
> Will enter joyful and happy into heaven;
> Heaven's angels will show felicity.

> The angels of heaven will show great joy;
> Never did they show more than on that day,
> Since they well see that solace and good company will increase for
>   them;
> May God permit that we may enter into that throng.

> *(El Rey de los reyes, alcalde derechero,*
> *Qui ordena las cosas sin ningun consegero,*
> *Con su proçession rica, pero él delantero*
> *Entrará en la gloria del Padre verdadero.*

> *La companna preçiosa de Xpo consagrada,*
> *Del padre bendicha, del fijp combidada,*
> *Entrará en el çielo alegre e pagada*
> *Rendiendo a Dios graçias e a la Virgen ondrada.*

> *Los angeles del çielo farán grant alegria,*
> *Nunca maior de aquella fiçieron en un dia,*
> *Ca veran que lis cresçe solaz e compannia:*
> *Dios mande que entremos en essa confradia.)*

The rewards of the blessed are enumerated by the poet. The rewards are numerous and what one would expect, and they are recounted with the ring of authority used by preachers who so firmly believe as to be completely certain. Moreover, the rewards would have meant a very good deal to medieval man, whose creature comforts were sorely limited even to the upper classes, and virtually nonexistent to the lower. Warmth in winter, coolness in summer, sufficient food and clothing, light, travel with reasonable speed and comfort, freedom from fear and persecution, shelter— all these and many other aspects of life commonplace to many moderns were unattainable to the majority of people in Berceo's day. He enumerates heaven's blessings:

> We want to speak of the first grace:
> They will have life without end, never will they die;
> Besides, they will be resplendent, I do not care to falsify;
> Seven suns would not shine as brightly as they.
>   (Quatrain 54)

The fifth grace is the best, he states:

> There will be a fifth grace which is worth more than the rest:
> They will be safe from experiencing any harm;
> A master who provides such a blessing for his servants,
> He is a true master, let no one believe otherwise.
>
> All will express enthusiasm in praising the Lord;
> All will know charity and love for one another;
> They will not hear noise, so peaceful will it be;
> Nor will they behold clouds which are tempestuous.
>   (Quatrains 58–59)

The poem draws to a close with a reiteration of the fearfulness of Judgment Day when all—the saint and the sinner—will tremble before their fates are clarified:

> The Day of Judgment is much to be dreaded,
> More, indeed, than anything else could be:
> Each mortal will have his sins laid bare;
> Not one jot of his evil can he conceal.
>
> Everything that one did, the insignificant and the important,
> Unless he had washed it away through penitence,
> All, open to the eye, in the midst of the marketplace,
> Will be made known to all; it will not be hidden from them.

> *(El dia del juiçio mucho es de temer,*
> *Mas que ninguna cosa que podiesse seer:*
> *Avrá omne sus males ante si a traer,*
> *Non podrá nulla cosa de su mal esconder.*
>
> *Todo quanto que fizo menudo e granado,*
> *Fuera si penitençia lo ovo deslavado,*
> *Todo será a ojo en medio del mercado:*
> *Conosçerlo an todos, non lis será çelado.)*
>   (Quatrains 69–70)

Berceo ends the poem in two quatrains (numbers 75–76) into which he compresses an oft-repeated moralization, one filled with the threat of hell, but one aglow with the hope and promise of paradise. The last quatrain offers the keys to the kingdom, and as one would expect in a poem by Berceo, the Blessed Virgin is numbered among these keys:

> All of us who are Christians and believe in Jesus Christ,
> If we wish to free ourselves of these portents,
> Let us improve our lives, let us be penitent,
> Let us obtain glory, and avoid wickedness.
>
> Let us say our paternosters, in order to earn this,
> Let us praise the Glorious Virgin, let us beg grace of Her,
> Let us all sing "Ave María" in Her honor,
> So that we may reign with Her Son and with Her.
>
> *(Los qui somos xpianos e en Xpo creemos,*
> *Si estas visiones scusarlas queremos,*
> *Meioremos las vidas, penitençias tomemos,*
> *Ganaremos la gloria, el mal escusaremos.*
>
> *Digamos pater noster, que nos esto ganemos,*
> *Laudemos a la Gloriosa, merçet nos li clamemos:*
> *Todos Ave Maria a su honor cantemos*
> *Que nos con el su fijo et con ella regnemos.)*
>   (Quatrains 76–77)

V *The Hymns*

Three *Hymnos (Hymns)*[16] are attributed to Gonzalo de Berceo. Each is written in the *mester de clerecía* and each is a song of praise to a member of the Hierarchy of Heaven. In one, the poet lifts up his voice to the Holy Spirit; in the second he addresses the Blessed Virgin; the third is to Our Lord Jesus. All three are composed of seven stanzas, each of the usual Bercean monorhymed quatrain, a number long an integral part of Christian symbolism.

The sources of the three are well-known hymns written in Medieval Latin, widely circulated across Christendom. Berceo, as was his custom, used known Latin sources, translating their content into Spanish, but enlarging upon the original as he Hispanified and versified it.

The first hymn can be given a title from the wording of its first line, *Veni Creator Spiritus (Come Creator Spirit)*. It comes from the ancient Latin hymn known as *Veni, Sancte Spiritus (Come, Holy Spirit)*, a title also drawn from the first line. The author of the original Latin was probably no less a personage than Pope Innocent III (*ca.* 1160–1216), who became pope in 1216. His name is connected with several hymns whose authorship is uncertain. Berceo in his Spanish version follows the thread of Innocent's meaning, but does not translate as closely as he does in the other two hymns. This may very well be due to the fact that several versions or renditions of Pope Innocent's hymn were in circulation by the thirteenth century and that the Spanish poet followed a version different from the one which survives. This is a likely supposition in view of the fact that both the other hymns follow the Latin sources so closely.

The second, whose title, from its first line, is *Ave Sancta María, Estrella de la Mar (Hail Holy Mary, Star of the Sea)*, comes from the Latin hymn *Ave Maris Stella (Hail Star of the Sea)*, of unknown authorship. This hymn is known to have been sung as early as the ninth century, since a manuscript of St. Gall exists from that period. This is the most famous and most widely disseminated of the multitude of hymns written in honor of the Virgin Mary.[17] The meter in Latin is trochaic dimeter, composed of three trochees in seven stanzas, the same number as is the Bercean counterpart.

The third of Berceo's hymns, his *Tu, Christe, Que Luz Eres*

(Thou, Christ, Who Art Light), is the Spanish poet's rendition of the famous Latin hymn *Christe, qui Lux Es et Dies (Christ, Who Art Light and Day)*, also in seven stanzas.

The best way to understand the beauty of the content of Berceo's hymns is to read one in the original Spanish.[18] But content can be given, also, in a translation. The hymn chosen for this is the third:

Tu Christe Que Luz Eres
(Thou Christ Who Art Light)

I

Thou, Christ, Who art the light which brightens the day,
Who takest away the darkness, Who banishest it,
Well do I know that Thou art the light: illuminate my soul,
Thou Who preachest light and all good works.

(Tu Christe que luz eres, que alumnas el dia,
Que tuelles las tinieblas, façeslas ir su via,
Bien creo que luz eres, lumne de alma mia,
E que predigas lumne e toda bien fetria.)

II

Lord and Holy Father, of Thee we beg grace;
By Thee let us be protected in this darkness,
That we may rest secure from our foes;
Let those of us redeemed by Thee have a calm night.

(Sennor e Padre Sancto, a ti merçet pedimos,
Por ti en esta noche seamos defendidos
Que folguemos seguros de nuestros enemigos,
Ayamos noche buena los de ti redemidos.)

III

Let us not be tempted by the dream of evil things;
Let us not be blackened by the wicked enemy;
Give not our flesh to the King of Devils,
Who giveth evil counsel, both filthy and venomous.

(De suenno de part mala non seamos tentados,
Del enemigo malo non seamos hollados,
Non consienta la carne al rey de los pecados,
Que da malos conseios, suçios e enconados.)

IV

Let our eyes know sleep, as is natural;
Let our hearts keep watch, this is meet;
Let Thy right hand with great patience defend
The servant who loveth Thee, who offereth prayers before Thy face.

(Los oios prendan suenno, commo es su natura,
Los corazones velen, esto es derechura:
Defienda la tu diestra sancta de grant mesura
Los siervos que te aman, oran la tu figura.)

V

Cast Thine eyes upon us, Defending Lord;
Preserve us from the Devil, an evil scourge:
Rule Thy servants, as a good governor,
Whom Thou, in great agony, bought with Thy blood.

(Torna a nos tus oios, tu, nuestro defensor,
Refieri al diablo, un mal envaidor,
Gobierna los tus siervos, tu, buen gobernador,
Los que con la tu sangre comprast con grant dolor.)

VI

Lord, remember us, deign to defend us
So that our flesh may not confound our spirits;
Lord, Who for our souls wished to suffer Passion,
Forsake us not, nor wish to damn us.

(Sennor, de nos te miembre, denna nos defender
Que non pueda la carne la alma confonder:
Sennor que por las almas quisist passion prender,
Tu non nos desampares, nin nos desses perder.)

VII

Thou, Father in Heaven, Almighty,
With the Son, than Thee, no less mighty,
And with the Holy Ghost filled with grace,
Give us a perfect death, a good shelter for our souls. Amen.

(Tu, Padre de los çielos en todo poderoso,
Con el Fijo qual tu non menos poderoso,
E con el Spiritu Sancto de donos graçioso,
Tu nos da fin perfecta, a las almas buen poso. Amen.)

These hymns, all but forgotten and seldom even mentioned today in histories of Spanish literature, deserve a place in the repertory of Gonzalo de Berceo's contributions. They are the equal of hymns in the vernaculars of many lands, and in quality are favorably comparable to other hymns in medieval Spanish. It is a pity that no musical notations accompany them.

CHAPTER 8

Summation

GONZALO de Berceo lived and wrote in a period of cultural expansion and ecclesiastical retrenchment. The cultural ferment owed to the interest and activities of such monarchs as Ferdinand III of Castile and Leon (1230–1252) had no noticeable impact upon Berceo's writing, although he seems to have been aware of some of what was happening. The poet was not completely ignorant of Spanish history, and was apparently able to comment with considerable accuracy upon various rulers and upon geographical locations in the Peninsula. He mentions, it will be recalled, rulers of earlier times, such as García of Navarre, Ferdinand I and Alfonso VI of Castile, together with some of the battles they fought. When he mentions towns or cities or monastic houses, he places these in their correct geographical locales, and some, like Toledo, he obviously had visited.

The ecclesiastical retrenchment, on the other hand, affected him greatly and served, at least partially, to motivate some of his writings—this especially as regards his *Vidas*. The Church was active in strengthening its sway and in reaching the people through a revival of interest in local as well as international shrines. Berceo took part in these efforts and much of his literary contribution falls into the category of saints' lives and miracles of the local saints and of the Virgin Mary. Writing with deep religious zeal and pious devotion about Our Lady, about San Millán, about Santo Domingo, about Santa Oria, and about St. Laurencio, Berceo evolved a personal touch not well developed before his time. Through this he most probably established a strong rapport with his public. If some of this devotion stimulated the poet to write religious propaganda to persuade wayward parishioners to pay the sums of money they had vowed and to enrich the coffers of local monasteries thereby, we can believe that true piety was at the root of such motivation.

Berceo apparently respected and loved the people and realized that untutored folk lived in perplexity and confusion concerning doctrinal matters. This seems to have been his reason for putting into the Spanish language bodies of material found hitherto only in Latin, so that the people could obtain a clearer understanding. His poetic and sometimes naive explanations of matters like the *Sacrifice of the Mass* and the *Signs to Appear before Judgment Day* are simplifications and popularizations of these doctrinal and scriptural subjects.

Although viewed by some scholars as a simple cleric, a delightful primitive, a rhymer, and an unsophisticated raconteur of pious tales—all of which he may have been—he should be seen also as something more. He was, too, a clever and facile poet with a keen and witty mind and a driving purpose, that of teaching his unsophisticated contemporaries what he thought they should know about matters religious.

Berceo's art does not point to special training of the sort offered in many medieval universities, nor does it preclude the possibility of special training. Well-known tracts or books of instruction dealing with poetic techniques were, of course, extant in the thirteenth century, and Berceo could have had access to such books, or might have talked to clerics who had read and studied such arts of poetry. Berceo could, then, have learned something of stylistics and techniques from books, but like most poets, then and now, he quite probably followed his own tendencies and rules. Although he did use a style of verse, *cuaderna vía,* or the *mester de clerecía,* he certainly did not allow strict form to prevent the spontaneous overflow of human emotion which is the bedrock of pure poetry.

Quite probably Berceo did not consult the current *artes poéticas,* nor did he attend any university where he might have engaged in the studies of "authors and arts" offered in the better medieval institutions of higher learning.

His works seem to be designed to please himself, his parishioners, and his brethren at San Millán and at Santo Domingo de Silos. The rules for poetic art in those days did not stress simplicity, the personal touch, and syntactical and lexicographical aspects closely associated with an author's region and dialect.

These are the facts of Gonzalo de Berceo's personality and purpose that give his works a certain immortality, these and his surprising insights into his own sentiments, his unusually vivid word pictures of his times and of the people who were his contemporaries, all interlarded with his refreshing turn of phrase and concept. The copiousness of his production is surprising, as is the vastness of his vocabulary and his diversity of syntax, all of which might lead one to state that his works could have helped to enrich and develop Castilian grammar.

Perhaps one of the most telling of assessments of him as a poet, a cleric, a human being, and a scholar, was set down in a poem written in a hand most probably not earlier than the fifteenth century, although possibly it may be a fourteenth- or even a thirteenth-century hand. Scholars have avoided this poem, fearful, no doubt, of the accusation of accepting a forgery or a poem deliberately contrived by some modern writer. The noted erudite, Don Tomás Antonio Sánchez, in his *Poesías Anteriores al Siglo XV*, I, 465–73, published this poem—it is a *Loor de Gonzalo de Berceo*—stating (I translate his Spanish) that "The following verses are placed here, as much because they contain a eulogy of Don Gonzalo de Berceo, as because also the versification, the language, the style, the simplicity, the verve and grammatical comparisons represent an antiquity equal to those of our poet. One could believe that the one who composed it could have been his contemporary except for the fact that the 11th and 45th quatrains indicate that it was sufficiently later, according to the meaning of the adverb *estonce,* which denotes a precedence on Berceo's part, of at least a half a century. This variety of meter ceased to be used, apparently at the end of the fourteenth century, or very early in the fifteenth, during which Pero López de Ayala, el Viejo, died. According to all this, who could be certain that this eulogy was not written during the first three centuries of Castilian poetry?"

Any interested monk who lived at San Millán or at Santo Domingo de Silos could have read Berceo's works and, from monastic records, could have accumulated the facts about the poet's life which were known. Some of the facts, or at least some of the ideas and suppositions inserted into the *Loor,* however, might have come from hearsay or from conversations with people interested in the local lore and history of the two monasteries. Also, the author of the *Loor,* who must surely have been a monk, might have based the statements he made in quatrains 4, 5, and 6 upon his own knowledge of monastic training. Or, the poet might even have seen Berceo as he worked at San Millán. Indeed, although less likely, the poet could have been Berceo himself writing his own autobiography.

Be that as it may the *Loor de Gonzalo de Berceo,* possibly composed by a Berceo anxious to perpetuate his authorship, or written by a contemporary, perhaps a monk of San Millán Monastery, or set down some centuries after Berceo's death by some other cleric, has some statements about the poet which are still applicable to the man and his works and which are fitting for the conclusion of this study. Of special interest is the description of Berceo's education. Quatrains 4, 5, and 6 describe some of the aspects of his monastic training:

> From the days of his novitiate he was instructed at the convent
> By those cloistered monks who cared for his needs,
> And they trained him well—long and carefully,
> They sowed seed in good land, they reaped a fine harvest.
>
> The holy monks, men of good works,
> Guided him along the paths and the highways;
> They pointed to the straight and level roads;
> God keep the souls of such good laborers.
>
> They instructed him in the Latin language
> Which he learned, little by little, to savor;
> They taught him likewise much excellent doctrine,
> Which was far more advantageous than chicken broth.

The poet goes on in quatrains 7, 8, and 9 to enlarge upon Berceo's education. This and the above-mentioned quatrains are the only description we have of it, and whether the result of hearsay, supposition, or observation, the lines are of great value. They describe medieval clerical training and round out what Berceo reveals of himself in his works. Quatrain 7 tells what praiseworthy instruction Berceo received from the monks:

> He who teaches the ignorant, who nourishes the needy
> Upon the holy food of the soul, that rich wheaten bread,
> Verily deserves to be the friend of God;
> He who does otherwise deserves not a wafer.

Quatrains 8 and 9, on the other hand, expand upon Berceo as he practiced his vocation, and portray him as he labored at his pious calling:

After the pious student had learned his Latin,
He toiled effectively among the monks;
The black-robed friars, men without malice,
Guided their student along a righteous path.

Master Gonzalo, in everything well indoctrinated,
Never forgot the holy vocation into which he had come;
During a long period he gave himself up to contemplation,
Beseeching Sir Christ to give him sound thoughts.

We read of his works of charity, of his deaconship and his entry
into the priesthood in quatrains 11 and 12, of his prayers for captives seized by the Moors and, in general, of his virtue, his piety,
and his industry. But more pertinent to the study and understanding
of his literary ability and his actual productivity are the next few
quatrains. Quatrain 15 of the *Loor* reads:

Many a good word issued from his mouth,
Which guided the blind, those erring folk,
And gave comfort to the weak always;
He gave many a cure to the sick.

and

Gonzalo de Berceo, most excellent cleric,
A most learned priest and intelligent man,
Wrote many a poem and many a ditty,
In order to provide folk with many a delight.
         (Quatrain 17)

At this juncture the poet treats most of Berceo's poetic pro-
ductions. Of the three *vidas* he wrote:

About Santo Domingo, that native of Cañas,
He composed a beautiful poem without any falsehoods,
A poem which relates his deeds, his miracles, and his skills;
This is worth more, rest assured, than a hundred chestnuts.
         (Quatrain 18)

He wrote about San Millán, that native of La Cogolla,
Born in Berceo, a work so superior
That every Riojan should have to learn it by heart,
Or carry it about with him to be read each day.

There is found in it how the saint won a good sum
When he drove from the battlefield the Moorish host,
Making that evil troop fall at his feet;
And through this he gained the donations, a famous reward.
    (Quatrains 19–20)

Likewise Don Gonzalo wrote a true history
Which recounts the deeds of the virgin, Lady Oria,
That black veil, from which the name Soria was taken,
He who reads it will find much gold and no dross.

The sister, Lady Oria, was named after gold;
She lived cloistered away in a convent,
Just as gold comes purified from the furnace;
Blessed be the parents of such a holy child.
    (Quatrains 31–32)

Of the *Miracles of Our Lady* we read:

Likewise from the miracles which the Glorious One wrought
He wrote another book of poetry very delightful;
The miracles are many, the account is very long;
But, even so, not all Her miracles are included in the book.
    (Quatrain 26)

Of the *Sacrifice of the Mass* we read:

Of the Holy Mass which is a sacred sacrifice,
Which That One Who gavest being offered to the Eternal Father,
He composed a poem so filled with savor
That it comforts the weak and drives out sin.

It pulls aside the veil from the Old Testament,
Unravels the mystery of that Divine Law;
And then it explains the New Testament, that Perfect Law,
Which Sir Christ, Son of the Queen, bestowed upon us.
    (Quatrains 21–22)

The poet refers to the *Duelo de Nuestra Señora* and to the *Loores de Nuestra Señora* also:

He had great zeal to be of the Virgin Mary
Her troubadour, and to write verse and in story

About Her Sorrows and praises which went beyond a hundred.
May Her holy devotee give us zeal.

Who would not weep, as he read of these Sorrows,
Beholding the Mother weeping close to the cross,
Staring at Her Son, watching Him die,
A sea of tears streaming from Her eyes?

He set Her Praises in such perfectly rhymed meter
That the value of many coins would not measure them:
The sadness which Her Sorrows suggested
Are changed to joys, when one reads the Praises.
      (Quatrains 23–25)

The poet did not overlook the *Signs Which Will Appear before Judgment Day*. In fact he became eloquent about this work:

As he read a most precious treatise which St. Jerome,
That great man, wrote about the Signs of Judgment,
He Hispanified a version in a noble poetic tract,
Which is a beautiful work, neither too long nor too short.

Short is the actual writing, though in all else it is long,
Because it reveals the Signs of Final Judgment,
Which will appear before that signal day,
In which Sir Christ, the Celestial Governor, will come.

On that day of sorrow no wretch will find
A corner in which to hide, nor a cave;
His face will be pale and will not be serene;
May Sir Christ shelter us and give us His Blessing.

Whoever ponders upon that Day of Judgment
Will separate himself from sin, will reject luxury;
You men who are errant, who cleave to fornication,
Cast yourselves straightway from such false pleasures.
      (Quatrains 27–30)

The *Martyrdom of St. Lawrence* is also duly mentioned:

He wrote in Spanish about the martyr St. Lawrence;
The holy personage suffered martyrdom in Rome;

They roasted him on a grill most cruelly,
At the behest of the Emperor Decius, a man of cruel mind.
(Quatrain 33)

The author of the *Loor de Gonzalo de Berceo* mentioned all of his works except the hymns, which, as has been said before, are attributed to Berceo with no certain authority.

Berceo wrote in literary veins definitely in vogue and, to this extent, was not original. In manner of presentation, however, he was extremely original and was able, through a remarkably personal and winsome injection of himself into his works, to establish an affinity with his contemporaries which has, indeed, extended beyond his own era and into our own times. Without this unusual rapport, his narratives in verse would have meant little more than the majority of religious tracts, saints' lives, and miracles, most of which are not remembered.

The last quatrain, number 44, reveals the eulogist's deep feeling of respect for Berceo. The quadruple repetition of the word blessed, in the pattern of the Beatitudes, emphasizes and drives home these sentiments. The full flavor can best be savored through the presentation of the original and the translation:

Beneytos los parientes de tan noble criado,
Beneytos los maestres de tan bon coronado,
Beneyta la villa do tal Fiio fo nado,
Beneyto don Gonzalo que fiz tanto dectado. Amen.

(Blessed the parents of such a noble son,
Blessed the teachers of such a good priest,
Blessed the village where such a son was born,
Blessed Don Gonzalo who wrote such words. Amen.)

These few quatrains sum up admirably the contributions of Berceo as a priest and a poet.

Notes and References

Chapter One

1. Many histories of Spain can be consulted for the backgrounds of the Spanish people. A concise, but very valuable and authoritative one is William C. Atkinson, *A History of Spain and Portugal* (London, 1960). For the student who needs a general study no book is better. The best of the longer histories is that of Antonio Ballesteros y Baretta, *Historia de España y su influencia en la historia universal* (Barcelona, 1943–48), in twelve volumes. Roman, Visigothic, and Moorish Spain all receive extended treatment.

2. See the excellent history of R. Altamira, *A History of Spain* (New York, 1949), which is an authoritative manual of Spanish history in one volume. The *Diccionario de historia de España* (Madrid, 1952), in two volumes, offers some three thousand pages of useful information.

3. The history of the Moors in Spain may be profitably consulted in A. González Palencia, *Historia de la España musulmana* (Madrid, 1945), and his *Moros y cristianos en la España medieval* (Madrid, 1945). The authoritative study of E. Levi-Provençal, *Histoire de l'Espagne Musulmane* (Paris, 1950–53) is the best of all.

4. The Introduction of John E. Keller and Francisco López Estrada, *Antonio de Villegas' 'El Abencerraje'* (Chapel Hill, 1964), pp. 21–22, offers some discussion of the coexistence of Christians and Moslems in Medieval Spain.

5. The excellent history of Antonio Ballesteros y Baretta, *Alfonso el Sabio* (Barcelona, 1963), gives virtually all that is known about Alfonso X. Its introductory chapters discuss in detail the reign of Ferdinand III, and even to an adequate degree that of Alfonso VIII.

6. The most available editions of these poems in Galician are the following: *Cancioneiro Portugues da Vaticana*, ed. of Theophilo Braga (Lisbon: Imprenta Nacional, 1900); *Cancioneiro da Biblioteca Nacional Antiguo Colocci-Brancuti Leitura, Comentarios e Glosário* (Lisbon, 1949–58); and *Cancioneiro da Ajuda*, ed. by Carolina de Michaelis (Halle, 1904).

7. The definitive edition of the *Lay of the Cid* is that of Ramón Menéndez Pidal, *Cantar de Mio Cid, Texto, Gramática, y Vocabulario* in his *Obras completas* (Madrid, 1944–45). The best translation is that of Leslie B. Simpson, *The Poem of the Cid* (Los Angeles, 1957).

8. The definitive treatment of these epic cycles is that of Manuel Milá y Fontanals, *De la poesía heroico-popular castellana* (Barcelona, 1959).

9. See the edition of Pedro José Pidal, "Disputa del Alma y el Cuerpo," *Diario Español* (June 22, 1856), 2–3; see the edition of Ramón Menéndez Pidal, "Elena y Maria," *Revista de Filología Española* I (1914), 52–96; and the edition of F. Morel-Fatio, "*Razón de Amor* con los Denuestos del Agua y el Vino," *Textes Castillanes Inédits du XII⁰ Siecle in Romania* XVI (1887), 368–79.

10. See the introduction to the edition by R. Menéndez Pidal, "Auto de los Reyes Magos," *Revista de Archivos, Bibliotecas y Museos* IV (1900), 453–62.

11. Among the books most important for learned proverbial writing are *Flores de Filosofía (Flowers of Philosophy)*, the *Poridad de Poridades (Secret of Secrets)*, and the *Bonium* or *Bocados de Oro (Morsels of Gold)*. The best edition for the first is by Hermann Knust in *Dos obras didácticas* (Madrid, 1878); the second, also edited by Knust, is to be found in *Jahrbuch für Romanische und Englische Literatur* X (1869); the best edition of the *Bonium* is Knust's *Mittheilungen aus dem Eskurial* (Tübingen, 1879).

12. The best edition to date of *Barlaam and Josephat* is that of F. Lauchert, "Historia del Rey Anemur e de Barlaam e de Josephat," *Romanische Forschungen,* VII (1893), 33–402; the new edition, based on the three extant manuscripts, edited by John E. Keller and Robert W. Linker will be published soon. *The Book of Sindibad's* extant Spanish text, the *Libro de los engaños,* edited by John E. Keller (Chapel Hill, 1953), was set down after Berceo's time, but he might well have read some earlier version.

13. The definitive edition of *Amadís de Gaula,* the fruit of a lifetime of sound scholarship, is that of Edwin B. Place (Madrid, 1949–69). Its Introduction gives all the necessary information.

14. For a lengthy and informative account of the continuing influence of Classical writing into the Middle Ages, Ernst R. Curtius' *Europäische Literatur und lateinisches Mittelalters,* which was translated in the Bollingen Series XXXVI of Pantheon under the title *European Literature and the Latin Middle Ages* (New York, 1953), is an invaluable aid.

15. The famous book of the Archpriest of Hita can be read in several editions. The most available is that of Cejador y Frauca in *Clásicos Castellanos.* A complete English translation exists, *The Book of Good Love by Juan Ruiz.* Translated by Elisha Kent Kane, Introductory Study by John Esten Keller (Chapel Hill, 1968).

16. The best edition of the *Libro de Alexandre* is that of Raymond Willis (New Haven, 1934).

Chapter Two

1. See note 15 for Chapter 1.
2. See note 7 for Chapter 1.

3. Antonio García Solalinde, *Milagros de Nuestra Señora* (Madrid, 1958), ix.

4. Brian Dutton, *La "Vida de San Millán de la Cogolla" de Gonzalo de Berceo* (London, 1967), iii-x.

5. *Prohemio y Carta al Condestable de Portugal* in *Obras,* edited by J. Amador de los Ríos (Madrid, 1852).

6. Tomás Antonio Sánchez, *Colección de Poesías Castellanas Anteriores al Siglo XV* (Madrid, 1779–1790); edition of Pascual de Gayangos in *Biblioteca de Autores Españoles,* Vol. 57 (Madrid, 1952).

7. Albert Lord, *The Singer of Tales* (Cambridge, Mass., 1960) deals in detail with the modern singers of tales in Macedonia, drawing parallels between their techniques and presentations and those of ancient and medieval epic-type poems.

8. Brian Dutton, *op. cit.,* xii-xiii and in detail in the section entitled "Los Documentos," pp. 1–9.

9. Joaquín Artiles, *Los recursos literarios de Berceo* (Madrid, 1964).

Chapter Three

1. All citations from the *Milagros de Nuestra Señora* are from the edition of A. G. Solalinde in *Clásicos Castellanos* (Madrid, 1958).

2. John E. Keller has discussed the rivalry between the shrines of the Virgin Mary and the famous Tomb of St. James in "King Alfonso's Virgin of Villa-Sirga, Rival of St. James of Compostela," *Middle Ages-Volkskunde, Festschrift for John G. Kuntsmann* (Chapel Hill, 1959), pp. 75–81; Evelyn Procter shows the surprising preponderance of lesser shrines of the Virgin in *Alfonso X of Castile, Patron of Literature and Learning* (Oxford, 1951), pp. 31–32; and John E. Keller, *Alfonso X, el Sabio* (New York: Twayne, 1967), pp. 73–78, treats the subject matter of miracles in the *Cantigas,* some of which deal with local shrines.

3. Among the beautifully illuminated manuscripts of songs and miracles of the Virgin are the *Cantigas de Santa Maria* of Alfonso X. (See the editions of Leopoldo A. de Cueto, Marqués de Valmar [Madrid, 1889], the definitive edition in three volumes of Walter Mettmann [Lisbon, 1959, pp. 61–64], and the black-and-white photo-reproductions in José Guerrero Lovillo's *"Las Cantigas," Estudio arqueológico de sus miniaturas* [Madrid, 1949]). The music of the same *Cantigas* has been edited by Julián Ribera, *La música de las Cantigas* (Madrid, 1922), but the more up-to-date and recognized definitive edition is that of Higinio Anglés, *La música de las Cantigas de Santa María del Rey Alfonso el Sabio* (Barcelona, 1943).

4. Not a great deal as yet has been published about the folklore of the Virgin in medieval Spain. Brief but helpful is John E. Keller, "Folklore in the *Cantigas* of Alfonso el Sabio," *Southern Folklore Quarterly,* XXIII (1950), 175–83, as well as his "Daily Living as Presented in the *Canticles*

of Alfonso the Learned," *Speculum,* XXXIII (1958), 484–89; of value, too, is Frank Calcott, *The Supernatural in Early Spanish Literature* (New York, 1923).

5. See the doctoral dissertation of Richard Becker, "Gonzalo de Berceo und ihre Grundlagen" (Strassburg, 1910), who bases his edition upon Ms. Thott 128 of the Library of Copenhagen.

6. The Latin text comes from the edition of Becker, cited in note 5. Carmelo Gariano reproduces it in his *Análisis estilístico de los "Milagros de Nuestra Señora" de Berceo* (Madrid, 1965), pp. 31–37, with the Spanish from Berceo. The translation into English of the Latin text is my own, and was translated especially for this study. The translation into English of the lines from Berceo were published with the translation of the entire miracle in *Medieval Age,* edited with an Introduction by Angel Flores, New York: *Laurel Masterpieces of World Literature* (1963), pp. 343–45.

7. Several editions are available for this *Vida.* The older and always-in-print version of Florencio Janer is found in the *Biblioteca de Autores Españoles,* Vol. 57 (Madrid, 1952), 38–64. A more carefully and scientifically prepared text, but out of print, is that of Fray Alfonso Andrés, O.S.B. (Madrid, 1958).

8. The best translation of the *Libro de Apolonio* is that of Raymond Grismer and Elizabeth Atkins (Minneapolis, 1936); the *Libro de Alesandre,* ed. by Raymond S. Willis (Paris, 1934), is the most reliable text; J. C. Marden, *Poema de Fernán González* (Baltimore, 1904) is the best edition of this epic poem.

9. See the treatment of the *locus amoenus* in *European Literature and the Latin Middle Ages* by Ernst R. Curtius (New York, 1953), pp. 183–85. See, also, Agustín del Campo, "La técnica alegórica en la introducción de los '*Milagros de Nuestra Señora,'*" *RFE* (1944), 15–57.

10. The Spanish text comes from the edition of Solalinde, previously cited. The translation is my own and is complete for this allegorical sequence. It is the first in English to my knowledge. Solalinde in his edition inserts titles for the miracles. The manuscript itself did not have titles.

11. This translation by John E. Keller comes from *Medieval Age,* previously cited, pp. 345–46.

Chapter Four

1. Dutton, Brian, *La "Vida de San Millán de la Cogolla" de Gonzalo de Berceo* (London, 1967), pp. 164–66, is a definitive study of this *vida.*

2. *Ibid.,* p. xi.

3. *Ibid.,* pp. xii-xiii.

4. *Ibid.,* with a detailed account in a section entitled "Los Documentos" which appears in his book's Primera Parte, pp. 1–9. Américo Castro, in *The Structure of Spanish History* (Princeton University Press, 1954), pp.

353–54, touches also upon the practicality of Berceo and upon his sophistication which some scholars refuse to see hidden behind a facade of simplicity.

5. Menéndez y Pelayo, M. *Antología de poetas líricos castellanos,* II (Madrid, 1940); Valbuena Prat, Angel, *Historia de la literatura española,* I (Barcelona, 1946), 75–76.

6. Menéndez Pidal, R. *Poesía juglaresca y juglares* (Madrid, 1945), p. 275, note 3.

7. Of great assistance to those interested in poetic structure is A. Valbuena Prat's *Historia . . . ,* I, 73; see also T. Anthony Perry, *Art and Meaning in Berceo's "Vida de Santa Oria,"* (New Haven and London, 1968), pp. 8–13, for a general discussion of tripartite structure in Berceo with special emphasis on such structure in *Santa Oria,* pp. 14–17; see also Frida Weber de Kurlat, "Cronología de las 'Vidas' de Berceo," *NRFH,* Vol. 15 (1961), 113.

8. Delehaye, Hippolyte, *Les Légendes Hagiographiques* (Brussels, 1906), pp. 110–11.

Chapter Five

1. Two editions were consulted, that of Florencio Janer in *Biblioteca de Autores Españoles,* Vol. 57 (Madrid: Real Academia, 1952), 39–64, and that of Fray Alfonso Andrés, a critical-paleographical edition (Madrid: Padres Benedictinos, 1958).

2. M. Férotin, in his *Histoire de l'abbaye de Silos* (Paris, 1897), treats much of the backgrounds of Silos and of Santo Domingo.

3. Castro *(The Structure of Spanish History),* pp. 358–61, points out that there is a special "approach in Berceo's recounting of miracles which resembles that of the Islamic Sufis of Andalusia, who, like Berceo, inserted themselves into the miracles as they related them, thereby giving a personal appeal to their accounts." Castro, of course, sees the influence of such Islamic writers upon Berceo, a belief that, while possible, has not been accepted completely by Hispanists.

4. Castro sees much of this as does A. Valbuena Prat, *Historia de la literatura española,* I (Barcelona, 1953), 78–93. So does T. Anthony Perry, *Art and Meaning in Berceo's "Vida de Santa Oria"* (Yale University Press, 1968), pp. 14–17. All scholars who treat Berceo stress this personal quality. Recall Castro's sentiments (see note 3 above) as to Islamic influence.

5. Brian Dutton's article "Gonzalo de Berceo and the 'Cantares de Gesta,' *BH,* XXXVIII (1961), offers valuable insights.

Chapter Six

1. The most up-to-date study of this *vida* is that of T. Anthony Perry, *Art and Meaning in Berceo's "Vida de Santa Oria"* (New Haven-London,

1968); the edition followed is that of Florencio Janer in *Biblioteca de Autores Españoles,* Vol. 57 (Madrid: Real Academia, 1952), 137–44.

2. Perry publishes Sandoval's prose account of Santa Oria's life in an Appendix to his study.

3. Perry, pp. 5–6.

4. F. G. Holweck, *A Biographical Dictionary of the Saints.* (London and St. Louis, Missouri, 1924). Reprinted in 1969.

5. Marcial J. Bayo, "De Prudencio a Berceo, El tema del Martirio, de San Lorenzo," *Berceo,* VI (1951), 5–26.

6. See Chapter 1, note 14.

7. The edition from which all quotations are taken is that of Florencio Janer in *Biblioteca de Autores Españoles,* Vol. 57, 90–93.

Chapter Seven

1. The edition used was that of Florencio Sánchez in *Biblioteca de Autores Españoles,* Vol. 57 (Madrid: Real Academia, 1952).

2. See the doctoral dissertation (Catholic University of America, 1933) of Teresa C. Goode, "Gonzalo de Berceo. *El Sacrificio de la Misa.* A Study of its Symbolism and of its Sources," and H. L. Shug, *Latin Sources of Berceo's "Sacrificio de la Misa"* (Nashville, Tennessee, 1936).

3. David William Foster, *Christian Allegory in Early Hispanic Poetry* (The University Press of Kentucky, *Studies in Romance Languages,* 1970), 34–5.

4. I am deeply indebted to my friend John Paul Boyd, whose knowledge of matters theological has helped me greatly in this section of the study of Berceo's *Sacrificio de la Misa.*

5. Foster, p. 37.

6. *Ibid.,* pp. 38–39.

7. *Ibid.,* p. 40.

8. The edition of Florencio Janer, *Loores de Nuestra Señora,* in *Biblioteca de Autores Españoles,* Vol. 57 (Madrid: Real Academia, 1952), 93–103 is the only available text.

9. *Juan Ruiz, El Libro de buen amor:* Edición y Notas by Julio Cejador y Frauca (Madrid: Clásicos Castellanos, 1913).

10. See the edition of Pascual de Gayangos in *Biblioteca de Autores Españoles,* Vol. 51 (Madrid: Real Academia, 1952), 439–42. The full title of the work by Don Juan Manuel is *Tractado en que se prueba por razon que Sancta María está en cuerpo et alma en parayso.*

11. See Note 1 for Chapter 3.

12. Another famous Spanish cleric wrote an entire tract in which he laid bare his sins (surely not actually committed by him) before his readers. He was Clemente Sánchez de Vercial, Archdeacon of Valderas. The work bears the title *Sacramental;* the Archpriest of Hita in his *Libro de buen amor,* likewise called himself a sinner.

13. Two fairly recent studies attempt to provide a careful treatment of the *Duelo* as to structure and sources: Germán Orduña, "La estructura del *'Duelo de la Virgen'* y la cantica *'Eya Velar,'"* *Humanitas,* Vol. 10 (1958), and José Oroz Reta, "Paralelismo literario entre el *'Duelo'* de Berceo, y el 'De lamentationes' y 'Los Evangelios,'" *Helmática,* II (1951).

14. Bruce W. Wardropper in an article which assembles the previous thinking of scholars as to *"Eya Velar"* and supplies his own opinions should be consulted. See his "Berceo's *'Eya Velar,'"* *Romance Notes,* II (1960), 3–8. Other articles about the words, "Eya Velar," should be consulted for a full understanding: J. B. Trend, "Sobre el *'Eya Velar'* de Berceo," *NRFH,* V (1951), 226–28; Leo Spitzer, "Sobre la cántica *'Eya Velar,'"* *NRFH,* IV (1950), 50–56. Both Spitzer and Wardropper believe that originally the word "eya" was a cry used to encourage oarsmen. "Just as a coxswain in a modern racing eight calls his long drawn-out numbers "on-óne," "Two-óo," so one may imagine "eya" sung with an extended first vowel and ending snappily on the sharp "ya." The sound would no doubt be effective as a jolt to jerk the guards out of their somnolence," (Wardropper, p. 6, note 9). From the cry issued to oarsmen, "eya" quite probably carried over into other cries for alerting other groups. For this reason we can logically call it a "watchmen's chant." It should not be forgotten, even so, that the *Thesaurus Linguae Latinae* lists many examples of *eya*—one even from *Salve Regina.* The cry, if it actually originated with oarsmen, must have soon been taken up by other people and used for other activities. I am grateful to Stephen Kirby for convincing me that the lines *Non sabedes tanto descanto . . . Que salgades de so el canto . . .* are addressed by the guards to the dead Jesus Himself. His forthcoming articles will strengthen this translation.

15. Berceo's humor, sometimes simple and direct, sometimes wry, has been much discussed. The article by Georges Cirot, "L'humour de Berceo," *Bulletin of Hispanic Studies,* XLIV (1942), 160–65, is well worth consulting, as is the same writer's "L'expression dans Gonzalo de Berceo," *RFE,* IX (1922), 54–70.

16. See the edition of Florencio Janer in *Biblioteca de Autores Españoles,* Vol. 57 (Madrid: Real Academia, 1952), 144.

17. See Erasmo Buceta, "Sobre una paranomasia en Gonzalo de Berceo," *RFE,* VIII (1921), 63–64.

18. See note 16.

Selected Bibliography

PRIMARY SOURCES

1. Editions of Berceo's Works

Milagros de Nuestra Señora. Edition by A. [García] Solalinde in *Clásicos Castellanos* (Madrid, 1958). *Los Milagros de Nuestra Señora*. Edition of Florencio Janer in *Biblioteca de Autores Españoles*, Vol. 57 (Madrid: Real Academia, 1952), 103–31. C. Carrol Marden, *Veintitrés Milagros: Nuevo Manuscrito de la Real Academia Española* (Madrid: Hernando, 1929). A. Hämel's edition of *Milagros de Nuestra Señora* (Halle: Niemeyer, 1926) has a good introduction in German but contains only seventeen of the miracles.

Vida de Santo Domingo de Silos. Edition of Florencio Janer in *Biblioteca de Autores Españoles*, Vol. 57 (Madrid, 1952), 39–64. Fray Alfonso Andrés, *Vida de Santo Domingo de Silos*. Edición Críticopaleográfica del Códice del Siglo XIII (Madrid: Padres Benedictinos, 1958). *Vida de Santo Domingo de Silos*. Edition critique publiée par John D. Fitzgerald. (Paris: E. Bouillon, 1904).

Vida de San Millán de la Cogolla. Edition of Brian Dutton (London: Tamesis Books, 1967). Edition of Florencio Janer in *Biblioteca de Autores Españoles*, Vol. 57 (Madrid, 1952), 65–79. Dutton's edition is the more scientific and scholarly, but Janer's has always been available and will stay in print.

Vida de Santa Oria. Edition of Florencio Janer in *Biblioteca de Autores Españoles*, Vol. 57 (Madrid, 1942), 137–44.

MARDEN, CHARLES CARROL. "Martirio de San Lorenzo," from an Unpublished Manuscript, *PMLA*, XLV (1930), 501–15.

Martyrio de San Laurencio. Edition of Florencio Janer in *Biblioteca de Autores Españoles*, Vol. 57 (Madrid, 1952), 90–93.

Duelo de la Virgen. Edition of Florencio Janer in *Biblioteca de Autores Españoles*, Vol. 57 (Madrid: Real Academia, 1952), 131–37.

Loores de Nuestra Señora. Edition of Florencio Janer in *Biblioteca de Autores Españoles*, Vol. 57 (Madrid: Real Academia, 1952), 93–103.

Sacrificio de la Misa. Edition of Florencio Janer in *Biblioteca de Autores Españoles*, Vol. 57 (Madrid: Real Academia, 1952), 80–90. *Sacrificio de la Misa*. Edition of Antonio García Solalinde (Madrid: Residencia de Estudiantes, 1913).

De los Signos que Aparescerán ante el Juicio. Edition of Florencio Janer in

Biblioteca de Autores Españoles, Vol. 57 (Madrid: Real Academia, 1952), 101–3.

MARDEN, CHARLES CARROLL. *Cuatro poemas de Berceo* (Madrid: Real Academia, 1928). Two *milagros* and the *Vidas* of San Millán and of Santa Oria.

2. Translations of Berceo's Works

The Archbishop's Chasuble and *The Ignorant Monk,* translated by John E. Keller in *Medieval Age,* Edited with an Introduction by Angel Flores, *Laurel Masterpieces of World Literature* (New York, 1963) pp. 343–44 and 345–46 respectively.

SECONDARY SOURCES

1. Doctoral Dissertations

BECKER, RICHARD. "Gonzalo de Berceo. *Los Milagros* und ihre Grundlagen" (Strassburg, 1910).

GARGOLINE, PATRICK. "The *'Milagros de Nuestra Señora'* of Gonzalo de Berceo. Versification, Language, and Berceo's Treatment of His Latin Sources" (Columbia, 1959).

GOODE, TERESA CLARA. "Gonzalo de Berceo. *'El Sacrificio de la Misa.'* A Study of Its Symbolism and of Its Sources" (Catholic University, 1933).

2. Books

ALTAMIRA, RAFAEL. *A History of Spain* (New York: Macmillan, 1918).

ARTILES, JOAQUÍN. *Los recursos literarios de Berceo* (Madrid: Editorial Gredos, 1964).

ATKINSON, WILLIAM C. *A History of Spain and Portugal* (London: Whitfriars Press, 1960). This is a remarkable brief history and one of the best, if not the best, for student use.

———. *The Classical Heritage of the Middle Ages* (New York, 1958).

AUERBACH, ENRICH. *Scenes from the Drama of European Literature* (New York, 1959).

BALBÍN LUCAS, RAFAEL. *Sistema rítmica castellana* (Madrid: Editorial Gredos, 1962).

BALLESTEROS Y BARETTA, ANTONIO. *Historia de España y su influencia en la historia universal* (Barcelona: Salvat Editores, 1943–48). 12 volumes. This is an authoritative work which places Spanish history in the context of world history.

BRENAN, GERALD. *The Literature of the Spanish People* (New York: Meridian Books, 1957). Readable, sound, up-to-date. One of the very

best general treatments of medieval Spanish letters, and especially
good for poetry.

CASTRO, AMÉRICO. *The Structure of Spanish History* (Princeton: Princeton
University Press, 1954). Provocative commentary. A controversial
study of many aspects of Spanish literature by one of the great scholars.

CHANDLER, RICHARD E. and SCHWARTZ, KESSEL. *A New History of Spanish
Literature* (Baton Rouge: University of Louisiana Press, 1961). A very
useful and reliable book. Literature is treated by genre rather than by
chronological approaches.

CORRO DEL ROSARIO, PEDRO. *Gonzalo de Berceo.* Estudio Crítico-literario
(São Paulo: Pia Sociedad de S. Paulo, 1933).

CROCETTI, G. GUERRIERI. *Studi sulla poesia di Gonzalo de Berceo* (Turin:
Paravia, 1942).

CURTIUS, ERNST ROBERT. *European Literature and the Latin Middle Ages*
(New York: Pantheon Books, 1953). An excellent English translation
from German of this important book. Curtius' is the most useful study
of the unbroken tradition of Latin literature in the Middle Ages which
was so influential upon medieval vernacular literatures.

DÍAZ-PLAJA, GUILLERMO. *Historia general de las literaturas hispánicas*
(Barcelona: Editorial Barna, 1951). This great work is a series of
studies by experts in the many genres discussed, brought together and
edited by Díaz-Plaja. Invaluable for concise and reliable discussions.

FISHER, JOHN H. *The Medieval Literature of Western Europe, A Review
of Research, Mainly 1930–1960* (New York: The New York University
Press, and London: University of London Press, 1966). This book
gives in Chapter 8 and in Chapter 10 comprehensive bibliographies
of Spanish and Portuguese medieval literatures.

FITZ-GERALD, J. *Versification of the Cuaderna Vía as Found in Berceo's
"Vida de Santo Domingo."* (New York: Columbia University Press,
1905). Probably the definitive work on *cuaderna vía.*

FITZMAURICE-KELLY, JAMES. "Berceo and other Forerunners," *Some
Masters of Spanish Verse* (Oxford University Press, 1924). General
but valuable.

FLETCHER, ANGUS. *Allegory, The Theory of a Symbolic Mode* (Ithaca, New
York, 1958).

FOSTER, DAVID WILLIAM. *Christian Allegory in Early Hispanic Poetry*
(Lexington: The University Press of Kentucky, 1970).

GARIANO, CARMELO. *Análisis estilístico de los "Milagros de Nuestra Señora"
de Berceo* (Madrid: Editorial Gredos, 1965). The most up-to-date
study on Bercean stylistics.

GONZÁLEZ-PÁLENCIA, A. *Historia de la España musulmana* (Madrid:
Editorial Labor, 1945). Concise, but authoritative and useful.

———. *Moros y cristianos en la España medieval.* (Barcelona: Editorial
Labor, 1945). A very good treatment of the two cultures.

GREEN, OTIS H. *Spain and the Western Tradition* (Madison: University of Wisconsin Press, 1963). 4 volumes. Masterly treatment of many aspects of Spanish literature.

HANSSEN, FRIEDRICH. *Metrische Studien zu Alfonso und Berceo* (Valparaiso: Universo, 1903). A valuable comparison of two important poets.

HASKINS, CHARLES. *Studies in Medieval Culture* (Berne: Franke, 1948).

KANE, ELISHA KENT. *The Book of Good Love,* with an Introduction by John E. Keller (Chapel Hill: University of North Carolina Press, 1968). The first complete translation into English verse of Juan Ruiz's *Libro de buen amor*.

KELLER, JOHN ESTEN. *Alfonso X, el Sabio* (New York: Twayne, 1967). The most extensive general study in English of the writings of Alfonso X.

LANCHETAS, RUFINO. *Gramática y vocabulario de las obras de Berceo* (Madrid: Rivadeneyra, 1900).

LÓPEZ ESTRADA, FRANCISCO. *Introducción a la literatura medieval española* (Madrid: Gredos, 1952). A desideratum for all students of Medieval Spanish Literature.

LORD, ALBERT. *The Singer of Tales* (Cambridge: Harvard University Press, 1960). A solid study of modern epic poetry against the background of ancient and medieval epic.

MIGNANI, RIGO and DI CESARE, MARIO A. *The Book of Good Love* (New York: State University of New York Press, 1970). This is the only complete translation into English prose.

MILA Y FONTANALS, MANUEL. *De la poesía heroica-popular castellana* (Madrid: Consejo Superior de Investigaciones Científicas, 1959). This recent translation of the French original is updated. Invaluable for an understanding of medieval lyrics.

MILLARES CARLO, AGUSTÍN. *Historia de la literatura española hasta fines del siglo XV* (México: Antigua Librería Robredo, 1950). This is the best general history of Old Spanish literature with chapters followed by excellent bibliographies.

NORTHUP, GEORGE T. Revised by Nicholson B. Adams. *An Introduction to Spanish Literature* (Chicago: University of Chicago Press, 1960). A useful, standard, and valuable work. One of the most up-to-date of such studies.

PERRY, T. ANTHONY. *Art and Meaning in Berceo's "Vida de Santa Oria"* (New Haven and London: Yale University Press, 1968). The most complete and detailed study of the *vida*.

POST, CHANDLER R. *Medieval Spanish Allegory* (Cambridge, Mass., 1915).

PROCTOR, EVELYN S. *Alfonso X of Castile, Patron of Literature and Learning* (Oxford: Clarendon Press, 1951). An excellent treatment of Alfonso X by an eminent historian.

SÁNCHEZ, TOMÁS ANTONIO. *Colección de poesías castellanas anteriores al siglo XV* (Madrid 1779–1790).

SCHUG, H. L. "Latin Sources of Berceo's 'Sacrificio de la Misa'" (Nashville, Tennessee: George Peabody College, 1936).

VALBUENA PRAT, ANGEL. *Historia de la literatura española* (Barcelona: Editorial Gustavo Gili, 1964), pp. 75–93.

3. Articles in Periodicals and in Books

ALONSO, DÁMASO. "Berceo y los 'topoi'" in *De los Siglos Oscuros al de Oro* (Madrid: Editorial Gredos, 1950).

ARNOLD, HARRISON H. "Irregular Hemistichs in the *Milagros* of Gonzalo de Berceo," *PMLA*, L (1935), 335–51.

AZORÍN. "Gonzalo de Berceo," *Al margen de los clásicos* (Madrid: Clásica Española, 1915).

BAYO, MARCIAL J. "De Prudencio a Berceo. El tema del *Martirio de San Lorenzo*," *Berceo*, VI (1951), 5–26.

BOUBÉE, JOSEPH. "La poésie mariale. Gonzalo de Berceo (1198?–1260?)" (Paris: *Etudes des Pères de la Compagnie de Jesus*, XC [1904]), 512–36.

BERNÁRDEZ, FRANCISCO L. "Gonzalo de Berceo como traductor de himnos litúrgicos," *Criterio*, XXVI (1953), 170–71.

BUCETA, ERASMO. "Un dato para los 'Milagros' de Berceo," *RFE*, IX (1922), 400–402.

CAMPO, AGUSTÍN DEL. "La técnica alegórica en la introducción de los 'Milagros de Nuestra Señora,'" *RFE* (1944), 15–57.

CASTRO, AMÉRICO. "Gonzalo de Berceo," *La Realidad Histórica de España* (México, 1954), pp. 341–50.

————. "Gonzalo de Berceo" in his *The Structure of Spanish History*, Chapter 10, pp. 35–161, translated by Edmund L. King (Princeton University Press, 1954). The Spanish title is *España en su historia: Cristianos, moros y judíos*.

CIROT, GEORGES. "L'Expression dans Gonzalo de Berceo," *RFE*, IX (1922), 154–70.

————. "L'humeur de Berceo," *Bul. Hisp.*, XLIV (1942), 160–65.

CRANE, THOMAS F. "Miracles of the Virgin," *RR*, II (1911), 235–79.

DEVOTO, DANIEL. "Notas al texto de los 'Milagros de Nuestra Señora' de Berceo," *BHS*, LIX (1957).

DUTTON, BRIAN. "Gonzalo de Berceo and the *'Cantares de Gesta,'*" *Bul. Hisp.*, XXXVIII (1961), 197–205.

FERNÁNDEZ Y GONZÁLEZ, FRANCISCO. "Berceo, o el poeta sagrado de la España cristiana del siglo XIII," *La Razón*, I (1860), 222–35; 300–322; 393–402.

FERRER, J. "Berceo: *Milagros de Nuestra Señora*. Aspectos de su estilo," *Hispania*, XXXIII (1950), 46–50.

FITZ-GERALD, J. "Gonzalo de Berceo in Spanish Literary Criticism before 1780," *RR*, I (1910), 290–301. Some ten scholars predating Sebastián de Vergara who study Berceo are treated.

GICOVATE, BERNARD. "Notas sobre el estilo y la originalidad de Gonzalo de Berceo," *Bul. Hisp.,* LXII (1960), 321–27.

GUTIÉRREZ-LASANTA, F. "Gonzalo de Berceo, cantor de la Gloriosa," *Berceo,* V (1950), 733–47.

HANSSEN, FRIEDRICH. "Notas a la *'Vida de Santo Domingo de Silos'* escrito por Berceo," *Anales de la Universidad de Chile,* CXX (1907), 715–63.

KLING, HJALMAR. "A propos de Berceo," *Rev. Hisp.,* XXXV (1915), 77–90.

ORDUÑA, GERMÁN. "La estructura del 'Duelo de la Virgen' y la Cantica 'Eya Velar,'" *Humanitas,* 10 (1958).

OROZ RETA, JOSÉ. "Paralelismo literario entre el 'Duelo' de Berceo, y el 'De lamentationes' y 'Los Evangelios,'" *Helmática,* II (1951).

REY, AGAPITO. "Correspondence of the Spanish Miracles of the Virgin," *RR,* XIX (1928), 151–53.

SPITZER, LEO. "Sobre la cántica 'Eya velar,'" *NRFH,* IV (1950), 50–56.

TREND, J. B. "Sobre el 'Eya Velar' de Berceo," *NRFH,* V (1951), 226–28.

WARDROPPER, BRUCE W. "Berceo's 'Eya Velar,'" *Romance Notes,* II (1960), 3–8.

Index